An Uncertain Future:
Thought Control and Repression During the Reagan-Bush Era

By Richard O. Curry

Preface by Norman Dorsen

Cartoons, Permission of Paul Conrad
Los Angeles Times

Published by the First Amendment Foundation

Published by: FIRST AMENDMENT FOUNDATION
                1313 West Eighth Street—Suite 313
                Los Angeles, California 90017

                (213) 484-6661 FAX: (213) 484-0266

Library of Congress Catalog Number 92-82816
ISBN 0-9627705-1-5

Book Design: Freedmen's, Los Angeles
Printer: Agency Litho, Los Angeles

IN MEMORY OF THOMAS I. EMERSON
1907–1991

THOMAS I. EMERSON
First Amendment Protector Tribute

Thomas I. Emerson, Professor Emeritus, Yale Law School, devoted his career as a Constitutional scholar and authority and his life as a humanitarian and activist to preserving and strengthening individual rights under the Constitution of the United States and the Bill of Rights.

He clarified and fought for the basic liberties set forth in the First Amendment and exposed the "wanton disregard for First Amendment values" demonstrated by both open and subtle assaults on those rights.

The Thomas I. Emerson First Amendment Protector Tribute extends Professor Emerson's contributions to American society through the granting of an annual award to a person or organization that most demonstrates active protection of First Amendment rights. Awards are decided by the following criteria:

1. Nominations for the Award are made by person(s) other than the potential recipient.

2. The recipient's actions have demonstrated an effective protection or advancement of the First Amendment or an element of it.

3. The basis or content of the action will result in a program or materials which can be utilized for educational efforts or continued action regarding First Amendment rights.

4. The potential for the award to continue or advance the thought or action for which the Tribute is given.

Proposals for candidates for the Protector Tribute may be made to the First Amendment Foundation at any time and consideration will be given by a special committee of the Board of Directors.

All recommendations, with supporting information, should be sent to:

FIRST AMENDMENT FOUNDATION
1313 W. 8th St., Suite 313, Los Angeles, CA 90017
Telephone (213) 484-6661

Table of Contents

Preface

This is a chilling tale, or rather several tales. In lean and often understated prose, Richard Curry details how our government for twelve years has flouted the law, shown contempt for it. Whether we examine restrictions on art or civil rights, internal security investigations or restraints on the press, the ''war on drugs'' or dilution of habeas corpus, secret laws or secret government, litmus tests for Supreme Court Justices or intimidation of potential whistle blowers, the pattern is the same: invasion of individual rights and a centralization of executive power.

The techniques of the Reagan-Bush Administrations for achieving these ends have been varied, as Anthony Lewis discussed in a recent column: Put people in charge of programs who will try to destroy them; shift power to agencies under White House control (e.g., Dan Quayle's Council on Competitiveness); privatize foreign policy by inducing rich foreign powers to put up funds (e.g., to supply arms to the contras); and even take over Congress's war power. Inventive minds have worked hard to conceive such ploys that undercut the rule of law.

Why have they acted in this way? After all, the President and his merry men (there are comparatively few women in key places) are firmly established in American society, in no sense marginal. They know, or at least were taught, about the nation's roots in the Enlightenment and its tradition of individual liberty. What leads such people to follow the alternate route, a reactionary and authoritarian tradition that also has persisted throughout our history?

No doubt several influences are at work, but in my opinion the chief cause is unreasoning fear. Fear of loss of social status at home; fear of uncontrolled governments abroad; fear of the rising influence of women and racial minorities; fear of religious dissenters; and fear of regulation of business enterprise. The attitudes are unreasoning because, as recent history shows, there is no necessary correlation between change in domestic and international life, even fundamental change, and the security and prosperity of Americans, including conservative Americans.

Whatever the reasons, there surely has been a shocking degree of repression, often lawless repression, since 1981. Such governmental excess not only dishonors the most moral strain in American society, but it can backfire. Justice Louis Brandeis understood this, writing in 1928:

"In a government of laws, existence of the government will be imperilled if it fails to observe the law scrupulously. Our Government is the potent, the omnipresent teacher. For good or for ill, it teaches the whole people by its example. . . . If the government becomes a lawbreaker, it breeds contempt for law; it invites every man to become a law unto himself; it invites anarchy."

If Brandeis was right, the very conditions that frighten people who regard themselves as conservative—lawlessness, anarchy, turbulence—will flow from the government violations that Richard Curry describes. If a whirlwind is eventually reaped, he has explained to us how the wind was sown.

Norman Dorsen*
Stokes Professor of Law
New York University Law School

*President, American Civil Liberties Union (1976–1991)
Recipient, "A Tribute to Norman Dorsen"—A Symposium; HARVARD CIVIL RIGHTS—CIVIL LIBERTIES LAW REVIEW, Summer, 1992

Acknowledgements

First of all, I want to thank Chauncey Alexander, president of the First Amendment Foundation, and the members of FAF's Board of Directors, for asking me to write *An Uncertain Future*. Among other things, the Foundation's financial support enabled me to engage the services of two gifted research assistants, Paul E. Teed, a doctoral candidate in American history at the University of Connecticut, and Gary F. John, a former student, a friend and a sympathetic, but exacting critic. Without their efforts and insights, the completion of this work would have been long delayed. My conversations with Alexander, who read the penultimate draft, resulted in adding material that helped to clarify several important points. My colleague, Vincent A. Carrafiello, discussed critically important aspects of constitutional law with me over an extended period of time. His own writings on drug testing, balancing tests, warrantless aerial surveillance and other topics, have increased my understanding of these issues.

I also want to thank my friend and associate, Donna Demac of New York University, whose books and articles on censorship have provided invaluable sources of information. I especially appreciate Donna's willingness to deliver her lecture, "The Magic Asterisk and the Broken Line: The Status of U.S. Censorship in the 1990s," at the University of Connecticut in late April 1992 "in honor of" my retirement after thirty-five years of teaching, twenty-nine of which were spent at Connecticut.

"Retirement" from state service is, of course, a wild exaggeration for a writer and professor. Not only will I continue to teach a course, on occasion, but am now free to devote far more time to research, lecturing, and writing on areas of interest—including civil rights and civil liberties. My family and friends will now have a chance to see more of me; and this includes Lil' Bear, our Australian shepherd, Max, our Labrador retriever, and E.T., our Mexican chihuahua, whose activities include playing ball, catching frisbees, taking long walks and swimming. Dogs, happily, are not impressed by titles, awards, and publications. Human beings have much to learn from the joys of companionship with canines.

Thanks also go to John Murphy and Karen Norton of WHUS-FM, who not only taped Demac's lecture, but later broadcast it over "Radio Free Connecticut." I also want to express my admiration for Richard Vengroth, Dean of International Affairs at the University of Connecticut, for refusing to provide a visiting CIA agent with a list of names of all foreign students on campus, along with their areas of concentration, the names of their advisers, and their countries of origin. Only if increasing numbers of principled individuals are willing to stand and devote time, energy, and influence to opposing the policies of the "New Leviathan" can we begin to look to the future with any degree of certainty.

Finally, I want to thank Deb Crary, who works for the UConn Research Foundation, who not only typed the manuscript with care but did so on short notice.

Photo by Roland Laramie, July 8, 1992

Richard Curry (center) and his research assistants Gary John (left) and Paul Teed (right)—pictured with some of the material used in writing *An Uncertain Future*.

Richard O. Curry

Richard Curry, a native of White Sulphur Springs, W. Va., received his B.A. and M.A. degrees in history and Hispanic civilization from Marshall University during the 1950s. In 1961 he was awarded a Ph.D. in American history by the University of Pennsylvania; and, in 1965-66 he was appointed a postdoctoral fellow at the Harvard Divinity School. Although Curry has taught at Morris Harvey College (now the University of Charleston), the Pennsylvania State University, and the University of Pittsburgh, he has been a professor of American history at the University of Connecticut for the past twenty-nine years. Curry has received numerous awards and fellowships for his research and writing. These include postdoctoral fellowships from the National Endowment for the Humanities and the Society for Values in Higher Education, an Award of Merit from the American Association for State and Local History, a Distinguished Alumnus Award from Marshall University, grants-in-aid from the American Philosophical Society, the Social Science Research Council, and the National Science Foundation. In addition, he was appointed Senior Fulbright lecturer in New Zealand (1981), and served as a USIA lecturer in the Philippines (1978) and in Australia (1981). Curry's encounters with USIA officials in Australia, which were characterized by blatant attempts at censorship and intimidation, led to the publication of a series of articles on freedom of speech including ''Paranoia—Reagan Style: Encounters with the USIA,'' and eventually to the publication of *Freedom at Risk: Secrecy, Censorship, and Repression in the 1980s* (1988) and *An Uncertain Future*. Curry is the author, co-author, editor or co-editor of eight other books including *The Abolitionists* (1965, 1973, and 1985); *Conspiracy: the Fear of Subversion in American History* (1972); *The Shaping of America* (1972); and most recently, *American Chameleon: Individualism in Trans-National Context* (1991) which contains a section on the transgressions of the Reagan and Bush administrations. In 1989 *Freedom at Risk*, which Curry edited and co-authored, received the Free Press Association's H.L. Mencken Award, and an Outstanding Book Award from the Gustavus Myers Center for the Study of Human Rights in the United States.

The Reagan-Bush Era
in Historical Perspective

Aims and Objectives

Most Americans like to think of the United States as an enlightened and progressive society. It is difficult to minimize the influence of the American Revolution, Enlightenment ideas, the protections afforded by the Bill of Rights, the advance of political democracy, attacks upon monopoly and special privilege, the destruction of slavery, and the implications of some social reform movements. Indeed, there is much to admire about American politics, life, and culture.

Yet, there is a darker side to American history as every informed person knows. We are not referring here to the truism that social progress is inevitably accompanied by conflict—bitterly contested encounters with conservative or traditionalist forces opposed to innovation and change. We are speaking, rather, of a reactionary and authoritarian tradition that is as deeply ingrained in American society and politics as is the spirit of light and progress.

This is not to say that American history is little more than a perpetual struggle between forces of light and darkness. Life is far too complex to be explained by simplistic exaggerations. Yet, this is precisely what some of our leaders, past and present, would have us believe. For example, Ronald Reagan, throughout most of his presidency, portrayed the Soviet Union as an "evil empire"—a godless, atheistic octopus extending its tentacles everywhere in remorseless efforts to destroy the "free world." Moreover, Mr. Reagan not only maintained that the nuclear freeze movement in the United States was infiltrated by KGB agents, but argued (before the onset of "Irangate") that opponents of his Central American policies, if not outright subversives, were "soft on communism."

The administration also denied visas to distinguished foreign visitors under the ideological exclusion sections of the McCarran-Walter Act, and labeled two Canadian films, one on nuclear energy and the other on acid rain, as "political propaganda."

In *one* sense, there was nothing remarkable about President Reagan's use of conspiracy rhetoric to justify a repressive "national security" program. From the colonial era to the present, many Americans, including prominent national leaders, have attributed the disruptions produced by war, labor upheavals, economic depression, and wrenching social change to subversives. At various times, Roman Catholics, Jews, anarchists, international bankers, labor organizers, Japanese-Americans, Communists, and others have served as convenient scapegoats for those groups and individuals who are unwilling or unable to understand the realities of a fragmented and complex world. In part, therefore, the Reaganite belief that "individual liberties are secondary to the requirements of national security" is part of a continuum that needs to be placed in historical perspective.[1]

Nevertheless, the policies of the Reagan administration also reflected *radical departures* from the past. This was revealed not only by the comprehensive scope of the administration's policies but by its ability to *institutionalize* secrecy, censorship, and repression in ways that will be difficult, if not impossible, to eradicate. This is true not because Mr. Reagan's perceptions and convictions reflected greater passion and zeal than those held by earlier countersubversive crusaders. The Reagan administration's success stemmed, rather, from *major structural and technological changes* that have occurred in American society during the twentieth century—especially the emergence of the modern bureaucratic state and the invention of sophisticated electronic devices that make surveillance possible in new and insidious ways. Although Mr. Reagan made effective use of "antistatist" rhetoric throughout his presidency in regard to domestic policy, he did, in fact, expand the power of the national bureaucracy for "national security" purposes in systematic and unprecedented ways.

The major objectives of this essay, therefore, include: an effort to place the policies of the Reagan administration in historical perspective, to analyze the implications of Mr. Reagan's policies themselves, and to explain why "the Reagan Revolution" is rapidly becoming a permanent part of the American institutional and bureaucratic structure. A major part of the reason is, of course, the election of George Herbert Walker Bush to the presidency. Although President Bush has not implemented any major new domestic policy initiatives, his decision not to rescind, change or modify any of Mr. Reagan's Executive Orders and National Security Decision Directives (which have the force of law), his veto of the Civil Rights Act of 1990, his reluctant support of the Civil Rights Act of 1991, his unsuccessful attempt to rescind affirmative action guidelines for all federal agencies, and his appointment of Justices Souter and Thomas to the Supreme Court clearly show that Mr. Bush's policies continue to fuel the aims and objectives of the Reagan agenda virtually without let or hindrance.

If the "end of the Cold War" has downgraded the use of anti-Soviet rhetoric so characteristic of most of Mr. Reagan's presidency, the language of demonology and subversion as applied by both Reagan and Bush to the "wars" against the international drug trade, terrorism, and organized crime, and indeed, Mr. Bush's desire to create a "new world order," provide justification for repressive policies that continue to undermine and destroy civil liberties at home. Phrased somewhat differently, President Bush has not proved to be an "innovator" but rather a "codifier" whose primary objective is to preserve and expand the agenda of his predecessor. The fact that Mr. Bush developed no coherent domestic program of his own, but vetoed legislation or threatened to veto legislation that overturned controversial Supreme Court decisions, or aspects of Mr. Reagan's domestic programs, illustrates the point nicely. The Reagan and Bush administrations' exaggerated fears of foreign threats and capabilities, their faulty diagnoses of major domestic problems which, in part, are rooted in a demonstrated hostility to the concept of an open society, bode ill for the future.

The Omnipresence of Conspiracy Fears

If fear of subversion, political hysteria and scapegoating is omnipresent throughout American history, this fact is not nearly so important as its virulence at a given point in time. The first important point to note is that such fears are most intense during times of national crisis—whether caused by international conflicts, domestic disruptions, or a combination of both. During World War I, for example, American citizens of German ancestry were treated as a potential fifth column. German language courses were abolished in some American colleges and universities; and the famed violinist, Fritz Kreisler, was not allowed to perform in Carnegie Hall. After the Japanese attack on Pearl Harbor, the West Coast was gripped by panic, and the government imprisoned thousands of Japanese-American citizens in internment camps in California, Colorado, and elsewhere. Senator Joseph R. McCarthy's erroneous but widely believed charges that government agencies, especially the State Department, were infested by Communist agents were, in part, a response to the tensions and frustrations generated by the Cold War.

Domestic crises, especially severe social and economic dislocations, have also produced conspiratorial interpretations that blamed foreign agents or alien ideologies rather than internal problems for social conflicts. The Populists, impoverished by the agricultural depression of the 1890s, believed that international bankers were engaged in a secret plot to reduce American farmers to peonage. Labor leaders, in the wake of the Haymarket Square riot and violent strikes that attended the rise of unions, were denounced as anarchists or agents of the Comintern. The Great Crash of 1929 was also blamed by some observers on the intrigues of international Jewish bankers.

A prime example of conspiracy fears resulting from a combination of pressures in both foreign and domestic affairs occurred during the 1790s. The Federalists and Jeffersonians took turns accusing one another of subversion. Jefferson's followers were denounced by Federalists as Jacobins who planned to bring the French Revolution's Reign of Terror to American shores. Conversely, Jeffersonians declared that the Federalists, who enacted the Alien and Sedition Acts, were monarchists bent on destroying the Bill of Rights.

Major examples of countersubversive crusades directed against purely domestic enemies are reflected in abolitionist attacks on the "great slave power conspiracy," Southern fears of abolitionist-inspired slave rebellions during the antebellum period, and the repressive measures directed by the Lincoln administration against conservative Northern Democrats or "Copperheads" during the Civil War. Even here it must be noted that the mounting sectional crisis during the 1850s caused many Americans to regard both North and South virtually as foreign nations; and during the war itself, "Copperheads" were wrongly regarded by Republicans as traitors who favored Southern independence.

Scholars have also noted that conspiracy rhetoric, accompanied by political, social, or religious repression, is also quite intense during periods when traditional social and moral standards are being transformed by rapid changes in the social order. Historian David Brion Davis has written two illuminating essays on the nineteenth-century American experience ("Some Ideological Functions of Prejudice" and "Some Themes of Counter-Subversion"), which deal primarily with anti-Catholic, anti-Mormon, and anti-Masonic rhetoric.[2]

In part, Davis argues that the open and competitive nature of American society inevitably bred anxiety and political insecurity. The very fact that the United States had democratic ideals and liberal institutions led, in times of foreign or domestic crisis, to exaggerated fears of subversion or betrayal. Since loyalty in American society could not be compelled, it had to be internalized. In sum, it had to be based on voluntary compliance since the United States did not have an elaborate national security apparatus until the mid-twentieth century which could, if deemed necessary, take extraordinary steps to maintain "public order" or protect "national security."

In the nineteenth century, therefore, "outsiders"—foreigners, Jews, Roman Catholics, Mormons, Masons, anarchists, and other "subversive" or potentially traitorous groups—were often subjected to harassment and violence not by government agents or prosecutors but by vigilantes. These groups justified their actions by using the vocabulary of demonology to protect their visions of public morality, public safety, or, indeed, democratic principles them selves. In fact, the reverse was true. Countersubversive mobs succeeded only in assaulting the very principles they professed to revere.

It may be objected that there were exceptions to the rule—for example, the passage of the Alien and Sedition Acts by the Federalists in the 1790s, and the arbitrary imprisonment of "Copperheads" by overzealous officials of the Lincoln administration during the Civil War. But even in these instances, considering the absence of a highly centralized, bureaucratic state, the effects of political repression proved to be temporary aberrations that established no long-range precedents.

Some scholars, in attempting to gauge the significance of countersubversive movements in American politics, believe that attacks on "conspiracy" in high places are little more than a sham, a crude tactic designed to discredit political opponents whose domestic policies are the real target. Thus, Federalists, who opposed Jefferson's social and economic ideas, tried to link him with atheism and the French Reign of Terror. More recently, Republican opponents of the New Deal hoped to drive the Democrats from power by accusing them of advocating "creeping socialism," selling out Nationalist China, or appointing avowed Communists to high public office. In short, the cynical use of conspiracy rhetoric by unscrupulous politicians provides a partial explanation for its public appeal in some instances. However, such tactics cannot succeed unless large numbers of people fervently believe that Jewish bankers, Roman Catholics, Mormons, anarchists, or "evil empires" constitute a clear and present danger to American security and ideals.

In an effort to explain why these fears are endemic, many writers have utilized sociological and psychological theories as analytic tools. Franz Neumann, Gordon Allport, and Erich Fromm, for example, emphasize the importance of societal disruption, alienation, and personality disorders in accounting for the success of demonic appeals in both the United States and Europe. Whether or not demagogues believe in the reality of the subversive activities they excoriate is not as important as their role as catalysts. In short, attributing personal or societal defects to scapegoats provides a psychological defense mechanism that allows individuals to rationalize failure by externalizing it. Germany, so the story goes, did not lose World War I because its armies were overwhelmed by superior forces. To the contrary. The nation was "stabbed in the back" by Jews!

The concept of status politics is another theory used by some scholars to explain the appeal of countersubversive crusades. Seymour Martin Lipset, a leading proponent of this approach, argues that status-oriented rhetoric "appeals . . . not only [to] groups which have risen in the economic structure . . . but [to] groups possessing status as well, who feel that various social groups threaten their own claims to high social position."[3] As a result, such groups relieve their anxieties and frustrations by concluding that conspiratorial groups occupy or are attempting to seize the bastions of power in government, the churches, the press, and the universities.

It must be kept in mind, however, that these sociological and psychological explanations of conspiracy fears are theoretical propositions that do not come to grips with all the variables required to provide comprehensive analysis. Such theories of behavior are open to the objection that they associate conspiracy rhetoric almost exclusively with right-wing extremism, and ideology is reduced to little more than subconscious rationalization, which is not always the case.

For example, the abolitionists before the Civil War and the Republican party during the war itself were groups that not only used conspiracy rhetoric effectively, but occupied the cutting edge in promoting revolutionary change. Moreover, many leaders of the American Revolution, as Bernard Bailyn has cogently argued, were convinced that the policies pursued by George III and his ministers were part of a gigantic plot to destroy the "rights of Englishmen" not only in the American colonies but at home. Thus, fears of subversion are not the exclusive domain of charlatans, crackpots, and the disaffected.

In conclusion: Countersubversive movements are pervasive in American society and have wreaked havoc on the lives of some groups and individuals at least once during every generation since the 1790s. At the same time, we have argued that attacks on alleged subversives have been sporadic and have not resulted, therefore, in any systematic effort to transform the United States into a "barracks state." If this is true, why then should President Reagan's dark vision be viewed in an even more forbidding light than the exaggerated fears of earlier groups who viewed historical processes through a conspiratorial lens?

The Growth of the Bureaucratic State

Earlier on, we mentioned the fact that the Reagan administration's "thirst for autocracy" (to use political scientist Walter Karp's phrase) benefitted not only from excessive zeal, but from *major structural changes* that have occurred in American society during the twentieth century. The most important of these changes is, of course, the emergence and growth of a highly centralized bureaucratic state.

Powerful government bureaucracies have administered the liberal domestic reform programs associated with the New Deal, Fair Deal, and Great Society programs; but the emergence of the United States as a superpower during the Second World War has also had major consequences. The advent of the Cold War, and ongoing conflicts with the Soviet Union and the "international Communist conspiracy" (e.g., Vietnam) created what President Eisenhower called a "military-industrial complex" that placed the American economy on a permanent "war footing." Equally important, the Cold War and America's role as the acknowledged leader of the "free world" resulted in the creation of an elaborate national security apparatus in the United States. This came about through congressional enactments, a myriad of executive orders and national security directives, and a series of Supreme Court decisions which, collectively, have downgraded First Amendment values whenever the government has invoked that magical concept called "national security."

Some of the functions of the FBI, the CIA, and other government intelligence agencies are legitimate. For example, the FBI plays a legitimate role in areas such as investigating organized crime and domestic organizations that employ violence in an effort to achieve their goals. The CIA, on the other hand, has a legitimate role to play in gathering intelligence information overseas. But the Watergate revelations, numerous congressional hearings, and information released under the terms of the Freedom of Information Act revealed indefensible and ongoing patterns of abuse—which we will discuss below—that threaten the existence of democratic institutions themselves.

The central point, therefore, is that the growth of institutionalized governmental power carried out by impersonal but entrenched bureaucracies has created the potential for implementing reactionary as well as beneficent policies. Governmental power can be used not only to promote social change, but to prevent it; and it can be used not only to safeguard the rights and liberties of Americans but to attack, undermine, and destroy them.

The Reagan administration, obviously, did not create the modern bureaucratic state, but its officials clearly understood how to use the enormous power at their disposal to promote their own domestic and foreign policy agendas. One of the ironies involved here is that the Reagan administration clearly understood that antistatist rhetoric had enormous popular appeal—and exploited it to the fullest.

Mr. Reagan struck a responsive chord by promising, among other things, to cut taxes, eliminate waste and inefficiency in government, bring escalating costs for social services under control, restore "free enterprise" to the marketplace through deregulation ("getting government off our backs"), close alleged "windows of vulnerability," and, at the same time, eliminate deficits and balance the federal budget.

The contradictions in the Reagan program were clearly recognized early on by foe and friend alike—for example, by former OMB Director David Stockman and former Vice President George Bush. The latter once described the Reagan agenda as "voodoo economics." Taxes and social services were cut, but military spending reached unprecedented proportions. The president's policies, in fact, produced $200-300 billion a year deficits which, combined with ever-increasing trade imbalances, threaten economic disaster. In sum, the Reagan administration, mired in its own contradictions, provided only short-range illusions, not long-range solutions to the complex problems encountered in both the domestic and foreign policy spheres.

It may be objected that President Reagan's policies, whatever their apparent contradictions, reflected the existence of a coherent ideology—a desire to dismantle the New Deal and Great Society programs, combined with a commitment to the most massive military buildup the world has ever known. If this is true, then Mr. Reagan's attacks on "big government" were highly selective ones. In fact, the Reagan administration granted such enormous power to the Office of Management and Budget under David Stockman and his successors that it became the most powerful government agency in our history. Moreover, the powers exercised by the FBI, the CIA, and the other intelligence agencies increased so dramatically as a result of Mr. Reagan's national security directives, it became increasingly clear that it was not highly centralized power that the Reagan administration objected to, but the objectives that governmental power was designed to achieve. The Reagan administration's extraordinary secrecy and censorship policies, combined with its massive assaults on civil liberties in the name of national security, were attained only by the arbitrary exercise and massive abuse of governmental power.

Some Reagan-Bush Policies Reflect Continuity

Even so, it is important to stress that *not all* the policies pursued by the Reagan administration were unprecedented. Many of Mr. Reagan's initiatives represented a continuation of the fears and "national security" concerns of previous administrations and the Supreme Court during the past forty years.

The McCarran-Walter Act, for example, passed in 1952 over President Truman's veto, was used time and again during the Cold War era to deny visas to foreigners whose views were considered dangerous to American ideals and values. Thus, the Reagan administration's decision to deny visas to foreigners such as Gabriel García Márquez, Patricia Lara, Hortensia Allende, and Carlos Fuentes—and indeed, its unsuccessful effort to deport the American-born writer Margaret Randall—should be viewed as part of a continuum although the Reagan administration's primary (if not exclusive) objective was to exclude critics, or potential critics, of its Central American policies.

In December 1987, however, Congress passed an amendment to McCarran-Walter (sponsored by Senator Daniel Patrick Moynihan and Representative Barney Frank) removing ideological reasons as grounds for excluding aliens from the United States until February 1989. In 1988 a new amendment was enacted that extended its application to foreign aliens for another two years; but it eliminated protection for resident aliens seeking permanent residence in the United States or who were fighting deportation orders by the Immigration and Naturalization Service (INS) in the courts.

Some observers correctly predicted that these actions were a prelude to the repeal of the McCarran-Walter Act itself, which in October 1990, was replaced by the Immigration and Nationality Act of 1990. The new act was widely hailed in some quarters as a major victory for Senator Moynihan, Representative Frank, and their allies who fought long and hard to eliminate ideological exclusion provisions from the new law. Unfortunately, this optimistic view was not merely premature but dead wrong. "Reports of the McCarran-Walter Act's death are greatly exaggerated," wrote Georgetown University law professor David Cole. "Its spirit lives on in the 1990 revisions." For example, immigrants can still be barred for mere membership in the Communist party; and it bars officials and representatives of the Palestine Liberation Organization. The law's language defining terrorism is so sweeping, Cole observes, that "the government could deport every alien who collected donations for the African National Congress during Nelson Mandela's visit, and Mr. Mandela himself would be barred from entering." It could even be applied to Chinese students who threw rocks at tanks in the uprising at Tiananmen Square.[4]

Equally important, the law also virtually provides the Secretary of State with carte blanche to exclude individuals whose presence involves "potentially serious adverse foreign policy consequences" without revealing the reasons for or evidence upon which such exclusions are based. The law states that such exclusions generally should not be based on lawful "beliefs, statements or associations," but permits it if the Secretary of State declares the foreign policy consequences to be "compelling." This authority, Senator Moynihan declared, "constitutes a deeply regrettable retreat from our efforts to expunge the cold war from our statutes." Professor Cole phrased it somewhat differently. "Far from repudiating the ideological litmus test," he wrote, "Congress merely adjusted [the new law] to today's paranoias. The national pastime of witch hunting did not begin with the McCarran-Walter Act, and unfortunately it will not end with its repeal."[5] Other examples that reflect continuity in American policy since the 1950s include the development of "balancing tests" by the Supreme Court, whereby the Court purports to balance the security of the state against the First Amendment rights of individuals. This is hardly a new phenomenon. In cases such as *Snepp* v. *United States, Haig* v. *Agee* and *Kleindienst* v. *Mandel*, the Court, in upholding the government's position, did not launch a frontal assault against First Amendment principles. It simply ignored them. In *Snepp*, for example, the Court ruled that Snepp's publication of *Decent Interval*, a book exposing the dishonesty, malfeasance, and corruption he had witnessed in Vietnam as a CIA agent, constituted a violation of a pre-publication censorship agreement he had signed despite the fact that the book contained no classified information. Snepp, therefore, was barred from speaking or writing about the CIA for the rest of his life without that agency's permission.

The Court, however, not only ignored First Amendment issues by viewing the case in contractual terms, but bought the prosecution's argument that Snepp's book had caused the government "irreparable harm and loss." The fact that the CIA had not attempted to enforce similar agreements against other government officials, such as Henry Kissinger, who had published secret information without permission, "strongly suggests," Judith Koffler writes, "that the real motive underlying the Snepp prosecution was the CIA's desire to silence arbitrarily a hostile critic."[6]

Moreover, the use of disinformation and psycholinguistic devices, such as misleading metaphors and euphemisms, to sway public opinion on both domestic and foreign policy issues is hardly unprecedented. Recent examples—for instance, Ali Agca and the alleged KGB plot to kill the pope, the alleged use of "spy dust" (mutagens) by the Russians to keep track of American embassy officials in Moscow, the mysterious Libyan "hit squads" which, somehow, failed to make their appearance in the United States, and President Reagan's public pronouncements linking Nicaragua with international terrorism, international communism, and the international drug traffic—were merely a few of the Reagan Administration's blatant propaganda efforts to mold public attitudes. In addition, attacks on the media, whether in the form of White House criticism, libel cases brought by Generals Westmoreland and Sharon, or diatribes by right-wing organizations such as the Heritage Foundation and Reed Irvine's Accuracy in Media (AIM), did not suddenly begin to germinate, flower, and bear fruit after Ronald Reagan's election to the presidency.

Finally, the new wave of conspiracy trials, which have taken place since the early 1980s, are reminiscent of the conspiracy prosecutions of the Nixon era whereby the Justice Department tried to intimidate or silence critics of the Vietnam War. The Reagan administration, however, added several new twists: the use of preventive detention, anonymous juries, "the armed courtroom," and the elimination of "justification defenses" which ofttimes led to acquittals in the late 1960s and early 1970s. A justification defense is, of course, testimony that allows defendants to discuss their motives in taking a particular course of action.[7]

The practice of preventive detention, authorized by the Bail Reform Act of 1984, has also been utilized in drug and racketeering as well as conspiracy cases. Traditionally, under our criminal justice system, a person indicted but not yet convicted of a crime, can be denied bail *only* if *"no conditions"* of release *"will prevent him from becoming a fugitive"* [emphasis added]. The Bail Reform Act of 1984, however, permits indicted persons (who are legally presumed to be innocent of charges against them pending the outcome of a jury trial) to be held without bail "if the government shows to the satisfaction of a judge that *the accused is likely to commit crimes, unrelated to the pending charges, at any time in the future"* [emphasis added]. The constitutionality of the Bail Reform Act of 1984, predictably enough, was challenged in the courts. But to no avail! In May 1987 the Supreme Court, in a truly astonishing decision, ruled by a 6-3 majority in *U.S.* v. *Salerno* that the act was constitutional. In rejecting the defense attorneys' argument that the act violated the Fifth Amendment's prohibition of imprisonment without due process and the Eighth Amendment's guarantee of bail before trial, the Court ruled that "the government's regulatory interest in community safety can, in appropriate circumstances, outweigh an individual's liberty interest." In fact, Chief Justice Rehnquist declared that "we cannot categorically state that pretrial detention offends some principle of justice so rooted in the traditions and conscience of our people as to be ranked as fundamental."

In a scathing dissent, Justice Thurgood Marshall declared that preventive detention was "consistent with the usages of tyranny and the excesses of what bitter experience teaches us to call the police state." The majority's decision, Marshall concluded, was, in fact "preposterous"—an "ominous act in [constitutional] demolition."

Big Brother Is Here

The Reagan-Bush Obsession with Secrecy and Censorship

Although we will have more to say about the use of preventive detention later on, our central point here is to emphasize the fact that the new wave of conspiracy trials during the 1980s (combined with the new tactics currently being utilized) reflects both *continuity with* and *a radical departure from* the history of the recent past. There are, however, numerous other policies first implemented by the Reagan administration (and now being enforced and extended by Mr. Bush) that were totally unprecedented. For example, Mr. Reagan's secrecy and censorship policies were the most sweeping in American history. The most highly publicized measure, the president's National Security Decision Directive 84 (NSDD 84), required hundreds of thousands of government employees and contractors with access to classified information to sign *lifetime* censorship agreements as a condition of employment. Such agreements, until recently, were required only of CIA operatives. As a result of opposition in Congress, President Reagan agreed to suspend, not rescind, this provision; but Mr. Reagan's agreement was nothing more than a subterfuge. The administration still required government employees to sign lifetime nondisclosure agreements under the terms of an earlier 1981 contract, Form 4193, as well as a series of similar agreements prepared by various departments of the executive branch. In 1983 alone, more than 28,000 speeches, articles, and books written by government employees were submitted to government censors for clearance.

In addition, President Reagan's Executive Order 12356 reversed President Carter's guidelines for classifying documents which were the most liberal in history—the culmination of a thirty-year trend toward reducing not only the number of documents classified but the levels of classification as well. Not only did President Reagan repudiate this liberalizing trend (which included the declassification of most documents within six years), but *reclassified* documents made available to researchers by previous administrations. The American Historical Association and the Organization of American Historians filed suit in federal district court in Washington challenging the legality of this practice, but, as yet, no decision has been rendered.

Even more amazing were the Reagan administration's unsuccessful efforts to classify research by American professors *based on unclassified information* whether or not such research was funded by the government, and whether or not the research in question was even remotely related to "national security" issues. Beyond this, private companies that collect nonclassified information for sale abroad—including newspapers articles and the transcripts of congressional hearings (in sum, information that is available in public libraries)—were pressured by government agents not to make such information available to foreign subscribers. These blatant attempts to censor "sensitive, but nonclassified" information may not be legally enforceable; but the ostensible justification for exerting such pressure was based on "mosaic or compilation theory"—the idea that nonclassified data may form part of a puzzle which, when pieced together, could jeopardize "national security."

"Mosaic theory" also served as a rationale for the FBI's Library Awareness Program which came to light in September 1988. Staff members at several major university, corporate, and public libraries in various parts of the country were visited by FBI agents who requested information about the reading habits of foreigners—especially those from Russia and other eastern bloc nations. As a result of a public outcry and hearings held by the House Judiciary Subcommittee on Civil and Constitutional Rights, FBI Director William Sessions informed Representative Don Edwards, chair of the subcommittee and a former FBI agent, that he had issued revised guidelines limiting the program to the New York City area. But, as Donna Demac observes, Sessions' assurances proved to be little more than "Bureau doublespeak." Not only did the program continue, but the FBI was soon "investigating librarians and other individuals who had publicly criticized the program."[8]

The Reagan administration also invoked the provisions of the export control laws—which were designed originally to prevent the export of certain types of technical devices or equipment—to prevent scientists from presenting papers based on *unclassified* information at international conferences, and this despite the fact that many of the papers involved had already been published.

In August 1986 the Reagan administration came up with still another initiative in an effort to control the dissemination of nonclassified information. The administration required all government employees with security clearances to sign Standard Form 189, an offshoot of NSDD 84. The form requires employees not to divulge not only classified information but that which is "nonclassified but classifiable." Steven Garfinkel, director of the Information Security Oversight Office, explained: "A party to SF 189 would violate its nondisclosure provisions only if he or she disclosed without authorization classified information *or information that he or she knew, or reasonably could have known, was classified, although it did not yet include required classified markings"* [emphasis added].[9] In the Fall of 1986 the government also issued SF 189-A which required government contractors, including researchers, who handle classified information to sign this form.

This new category "nonclassified but classifiable," may be as absurd as Catch-22, but employees accused of violating its murky provisions could be fired and prosecuted. Nearly two million federal employees signed the form "knowingly or blindly." Only twenty-four people refused to do so on First Amendment grounds. "Because of their courage and outrage," three government employee unions filed suit in federal district court on August 17, 1987, challenging the constitutionality of SF 189. As a result, Garfinkel announced that enforcement of SF 189 was being "temporarily suspended" pending the outcome of litigation.[10]

Unfortunately, the outcome favored the Reagan administration's position. After the three employee union suits were combined, their suit was joined by seven Members of Congress who also argued that a statute passed by Congress prohibited the implementation and enforcement of SF 189 and SF 189-A. In May 1988 a federal district court judge ruled that the congressional statute was unconstitutional. In July 1988 the judge further ruled that although SF 189 was constitutional, the phrase "unclassified but classifiable" required clarification. As a result the ISOO issued Form 312 in September 1988 which stated that federal employees and federal contractors with access to classified information were now required "not to divulge . . . unmarked information they should know is classified, to unauthorized persons." Such wording was, of course, a distinction without a difference.

As the litigation moved forward, Congress attached a rider to the Appropriations Act for FY 1989 that prohibited the implementation and enforcement of Form 312. As a result, the employee unions amended their suit and sought an injunction against the use of Form 312. The Justice Department, however, filed a motion to dismiss the amended complaint; and in March 1990 the district court ruled in the government's favor. Although the executive and legislative branches of the government continued to spar on the issue, the bottom line is that Form 312 remains in force. By late 1989 nearly three and a half million people had signed governmental nondisclosure agreements as a condition of employment.[11] These agreements are still in force and the number of people required to sign them, as a condition of employment, continues to grow.

The Price of Keeping One's Job

The number of examples illustrating the problem of secrecy, censorship, and repression during the Reagan-Bush era is virtually endless—a steady stream of rules, regulations, national security directives, executive orders, laws, court decisions and FBI initiatives and investigations which not only have the effect of "keeping America uninformed" (as Donna Demac phrases it), but are designed to harass, intimidate, and silence political dissidents and government employees. A few additional examples drawn from the Bush era must suffice in concluding our treatment of issues involving secrecy and censorship.

In 1989 the government produced an amended questionnaire that all government employees were required to complete. According to Gary Stern of the ACLU's Washington office, the new questionnaire stemmed, in part, from a bureaucratic desire to create one standardized informational form for all government employees. But clearly, the intent is far more sinister than that, whatever the stated rationale behind it.

Among other things, the revised form queried employees about drug use, treatment for alcohol or drug abuse and treatment "for a mental condition." And Question 30-A asked: "Have you every been a member, officer, or employee of the Communist Party?" In sum, the questionnaire suggests the existence of a new ideological witch hunt reminiscent of the McCarthy era, and it requires employees to surrender privacy rights as "the price for keeping one's job." Moreover, the new questionnaire applied not only to employees with access to classified information, but included groups whose jobs were classified as "sensitive." For example, the Bureau of Indian Affairs applied the "sensitive" category to all people who came into contact with children such as school teachers.[12]

A Proposed New Executive Order

In 1989 President Bush also circulated a draft of a proposed new executive order that would grant agency heads sweeping powers to deny security clearances to federal workers without providing reasons for such action and, at the same time, denying the individuals affected the right to respond. As yet, Mr. Bush has not issued this order. The reasons why are a matter of speculation. It may have been designed to intimidate potential "leakers" or "whistle blowers." Or the "end of the Cold War" might have eliminated the perceived need for it. But whatever the reason, it wasn't essential to achieve the Bush administration's objectives in the first place. In 1988 the Supreme Court ruled in *Department of the Navy* v. *Egan* that civilian employees of the Navy Department who had been denied security clearances were not entitled to an appeal. So much for due process.

The Ethics Reform Act of 1989

Equally disturbing was the passage of the Ethics Reform Act by Congress in 1989. This law, which went into effect in 1991, prohibited all government employees and officials (with the exception of U.S. Senators and members of their staffs) from accepting payments or fees for published articles, books, or public speaking appearances. The law applies not only to matters pertaining to official duties but to those completely unrelated to their work. In short, any government employee or official who published an article or a book, or gave a speech on gourmet cooking, flower arranging, quilt making, rock gardening or astrological forecasting could not do so for profit. The rationale behind the law was to discourage government employees and officials from devoting working hours to private projects.

In part, the Ethics Reform Act was designed to curb abuse. Former Speaker of the House Jim Wright, for example, in an apparent effort to avoid laws limiting campaign contributions by individuals, was paid excessive royalties for his book that had modest sales. Whatever the reasons, the authors of the Ethics Reform Act were insensitive to the fact that all Americans, including government employees and officials, deserve the right to pursue legitimate hobbies and independent projects for fun and profit without interference from government. Thus far, the constitutionality of this law has not been challenged.

Congress's Mixed Record on Civil Liberties

In light of the Ethics Reform Act, how does one reconcile the passage of this law with the fact that Congress vigorously objected to lifetime prepublication agreements required by NSDD 84, and passed laws on three separate occasions prohibiting the enforcement and implementation of SF 189, SF 189-A and Form 312? Moreover, Congress has consistently resisted executive branch pressure to pass an official secrets act, has refused to enact laws limiting *habeas corpus* appeals from convicted criminals, and prohibited additional aid to the Contras in 1985 by passing the Boland Amendment—a rider attached to the Defense Appropriations Act. Many other examples of enlightened action or inaction by Congress can be cited.

'Our central point here, however, is to observe that even though Congress has been far less repressive than the executive branch under presidents Reagan and Bush, and indeed a federal judiciary dominated by Reagan and Bush appointees, the Congress of the United States has been inconsistent on civil liberties issues.

For example, Congress has restricted access to certain types of information previously available under the terms of the Freedom of Information Act. It enacted the Comprehensive Crime Control Act of 1984 and Anti-Drug Abuse laws in 1986 and 1988 which contain repressive features. As we have seen, the Bail Reform Act of 1984, which was part of the CCCA, mandated the use of preventive detention. The constitutionality of this law, unfortunately, was upheld by the Supreme court in *U.S.* v. *Salerno* (the implications of which were discussed earlier). Moreover, Congress has also authorized the Drug Enforcement Agency (DEA) to seize the assets of suspected drug dealers, by the use of civil proceedings, who have never been indicted or convicted of a crime. Equally important, Congress has refused to restrict the application of the RICO laws (Racketeer Influenced Corrupt Organizations Act) to organized crime. Whatever one's position on abortion, the law, which calls for the payment of triple damages, clearly was not intended to apply to abortion clinic protestors in Connecticut, Pennsylvania, and elsewhere. In addition, the Crime Control Act of 1991 failed to pass—in part, because of a filibuster by senators and representatives who didn't think it was tough enough. And Congress has refused to enact legislation creating an FBI charter that would eliminate or curb some of that agency's worst abuses. Still another area where Congress has faltered has been its willingness to restrict NEA (National Endowment for the Arts) funding for projects involving "pornography." Thus, the record of Congress on civil liberties is mixed and problematic at best.

The NEA Controversy

The NEA controversy began in the spring of 1989. The photograph, "Piss Christ," by Andres Serrano, was displayed at the Southwest Center for Contemporary Arts in Winston-Salem, N.C., which is partially funded by the NEA. Serrano's photograph depicted a crucifix with an image of Christ submerged in urine. At about the same time, the Corcoran Gallery in Washington, D.C. canceled an upcoming showing of the Robert Mapplethorpe exhibit. The cancellation served to publicize the $30,000 NEA contribution to the national Mapplethorpe tour, and the fact that a few of Mapplethorpe's photographs dealt with homoerotic themes. The exhibit appeared in Chicago, Los Angeles, Berkeley, New York, Hartford, and Philadelphia without consequence, if not controversy. But in Cincinnati, city and county law enforcement officers delayed the opening of the Mapplethorpe exhibit for an hour while they videotaped the exhibit as evidence. Shortly thereafter, the Cincinnati Contemporary Arts Center and its director, Dennis Barry, each were charged not only with "pandering obscenity" but with the "illegal use of a minor in nudity oriented material or performance." After a highly publicized trial both Barry and the Arts Center were acquitted of all charges.

In Boston, Christopher Lydon, co-host of the "News at Ten" on WGBH-TV, taped the exhibit's controversial photographs for broadcast, and interviewed a panel of area artists on the merits of Mapplethorpe's work. One of the panelists admitted that she found Mapplethorpe's controversial photographs shocking—in part be-

A DAY IN THE LIFE OF ART CRITIC JESSE HELMS

Paul Conrad. Copyright, 1989, Los Angeles Times.
Reprinted with permission.

THOUGHT CONTROL AND REPRESSION

cause such work was rarely exhibited in public; but she did not find it to be pornographic or obscene. Lydon's program was a courageous piece of public programming as he chose to televise video closeups of the most controversial pieces at a time when Boston prosecutors were being pressured in some quarters to bring indictments against the Boston Museum of Fine Arts and its director, and at a time when conservative groups such as the Reverend Donald Wildmon's American Family Association, Pat Robertson's Christian Coalition, Beverly Le Haye's Concerned Women for America, Lou Sheldon's Traditional Values Coalition, and Phyllis Schafley's Eagle Forum were calling for the abolition of the NEA itself.[13]

The "lords of censorship" found willing allies in Congress. In July 1989 Senator Jesse Helms introduced an amendment to the 1990 NEA appropriations bill that prohibited the endowment from funding "obscene or indecent materials, including but not limited to depictions of sadomasochism, homoeroticism, the exploitation of children, or individuals engaged in sex acts. . . ." The Helms amendment, which became law in a slightly altered form, also prevented the NEA from funding "material which denigrates the objects or beliefs of the adherents of a particular religion or non-religion."

In the late summer of 1989, John Frohnmayer, an attorney from Portland, Oregon, was appointed by President Bush to become the new NEA chairman. Shortly thereafter, he canceled a grant to the Artists Space Gallery in New York because their catalog, printed for an AIDS exhibit, was deemed too "political." Strong protests from arts and civil liberties groups caused Frohnmayer to explain that the cancellation did not occur for political reasons but because of an "erosion of . . . artistic focus" between the time the grant was approved and implemented. In the end, Frohnmayer reinstated the grant—claiming that his use of the word "political" had been misconstrued. Even so, Frohnmayer instructed all of his program directors to send any application that might be deemed controversial to him; and he issued guidelines requiring all recipients of NEA grants to sign what became known as an "obscenity pledge." As a result many grant recipients such as Joseph Papp and Karen Finley, a performance artist, refused to accept their awards. Others, including writer William O'Rourke, accepted their grants but published scathing critiques of the NEA's restrictions in newspapers and magazines all over the country.

Frohnmayer's rejection of grant awards in June 1990 to performance artists Karen Finley, Tim Miller, Holly Hughes, and John Fleck, resulted in a successful challenge to the constitutionality of the Helms amendment in federal district court. Another important challenge to the Helms amendment came from the Bella Lewitsky Dance Foundation and the Newport Harbor Art Museum. These organizations received NEA grants, but returned their signed awards with the pledge against obscenity crossed out, and filed a suit in the Los Angeles federal district court. In January 1991, Judge John G. Davies ruled in favor of the plaintiffs—declaring the Helms-inspired obscenity pledge unconstitutional.

In November 1990, however, Congress had already enacted a new law (replacing the Helms amendment) which went into effect in 1991. The new law stated that "obscenity. . . shall not be funded" but left it up to the courts to decide the issue. In fact, the law used the Supreme Court's own standards by declaring that: "The work must appeal to prurient interests, depict sexual activity in a patently offensive way and be without serious political or artistic value." Nevertheless, the law also stated that if the courts found a work to be obscene, the recipient was required to return the funds and would be ineligible "for further funding until full repayment is made." Beyond this, the law concentrated decision-making power in the hands of the NEA chairperson. Peer review committees would continue to make recommendations, but their recommendations were not binding.

In 1991 Karen Finley and Holly Hughes, whose grant applications had been rejected by Frohnmayer a year earlier, received awards. Hughes, on learning of her award said, "this might get tossed my way, but I think that other artists whose identities are controversial—their race, their gender, their sexual orientation are just going to be weeded out."

But astonishingly, Frohnmayer unexpectedly changed course and adopted a hands off policy by the chairman in dealing with the recommendations of review committees. By January 1992 Frohnmayer was completely at odds with Congress and the Bush administration—declaring that he had become an advocate of complete artistic freedom. Partially as a result of attacks by Patrick Buchanan, who made Frohnmayer a political issue in the presidential primaries, he was removed from office in February 1992.

In mid-May 1992 Frohnmayer stated that his experiences at the

NEA had turned him into "a First Amendment radical." By this, he meant that he came to recognize that the First Amendment was not designed to protect popular ideas which don't require protection, but to protect unpopular ideas which do. Frohnmayer went on to say that he had been fired by White House Chief Staff Samuel Skinner on February 21 because of six lines of a poem "that contained an account of oral sex behind a church altar." The poem in question appeared in *The Portable East Side*, a small New York literary magazine that had received an NEA grant.[14]

Frohnmayer's replacement, Anne-Imelda Radice, lost little time in overruling the recommendations of her advisory boards by rejecting $10,000 awards to an M.I.T. art show in Cambridge and the Anderson Gallery of Virginia Commonwealth University in Richmond, both of which exhibited sexually explicit materials. Patrick McCaughey, director of the Wadsworth Atheneum in Hartford, Conn., said that both exhibits "seem to deal with serious and central issues. Both are in seats of higher learning. I am dismayed that that was not taken into consideration by the acting chairwoman." George White, director of the Eugene O'Neill Theater Center in Waterford, Conn., and a newly appointed member of the twenty-six member NEA advisory council, commented that it appeared that Radice is "going to be a decency czar."[15]

Former chairman Frohnmayer praised members of two advisory panels who resigned in protest over Radice's vetoes. The White House, he said, is dominated by "a conservative and, in my view, a destructive faction" of the Republican Party. But such news was undoubtedly cheering to the Reverend Donald Wildmon, who heads the American Family Association. On April 12, 1990 Wildmon mailed a letter to 200,000 people which included 3,200 Christian leaders, nearly 1,000 Christian radio stations, approximately 178,000 pastors, about 100 Christian television stations, and all 535 members of Congress. He urged Congress to abolish the NEA because, Wildmon declared, the "NEA has been insulated from mainstream American values for so long that it has become captive to a morally decadent minority. . . ."[16]

Obscenity and Censorship Cases on the State and Local Levels

Although the NEA controversies occupied center stage, examples of obscenity and censorship cases at the state and local level require attention. In Florida, for example, the rap group 2 Live Crew's album "As Nasty as They Wanna Be" was ruled to be obscene in 1990 by federal district Judge José Gonzales. Broward County sheriff Nick Navarro, without waiting for the record company's appeal to be heard, arrested a record store owner for selling the album, and the members of 2 Live Crew themselves for performing their songs in an adult club. In separate cases, the members of 2 Live Crew were acquitted, but the record store owner was convicted. His case is now being appealed.

Two years earlier, an Alabama record dealer had twenty-five rap music tapes confiscated by state authorities, and he was arrested for violating the state's obscenity law. According to the ACLU, this "was the first case in which recorded music was the basis for an obscenity prosecution." The record store owner was tried and convicted in a municipal court and fined $500. The owner, however, was entitled to a jury trial under Alabama law. At the trial, held in February 1990, the ACLU utilized the services of a music critic and a linguist as expert witnesses. Both testified that "such obscenity convictions would have a widespread chilling effect on artists." The jury acquitted the defendant of the charges against him.[17]

In Indiana, however, local authorities also went overboard by using the state's RICO laws as a justification for seizing the inventory of three adult bookstores which sold "obscene" books and films. After the seizures, the police padlocked the premises. In early 1991 the Supreme Court issued a combined decision in *Fort Wayne Books* v. *Indiana* and *Sappenfield* v. *Indiana*, ruling that Indiana's RICO laws did not apply to these cases. The seizure of the bookstores' inventory, Justice White wrote in the majority opinion, was a violation of the First Amendment's prohibition against prior restraint since the bookstore owners had not been indicted and convicted of any crime.

The list goes on. In 1989 a painting of Harold Washington, the late Chicago mayor, which depicts him in women's underwear, was exhibited at the Art Institute of Chicago. The painting so offended Chicago's Board of Aldermen that they ordered the police "to literally arrest the painting and remove it from the premises."[18] The painting was later returned to the artist "in a damaged condition." The ACLU is currently suing the city on behalf of the artist for damages and injunctive relief.

Besides this, there are literally thousands of school board book censorship cases nationwide; and, as a result of a Supreme Court's ruling in the *Hazlewood* case in 1988, school principals all over the country have been given the power to censor or prevent publication of stories they find objectionable. Mark Goodman, executive director of The Student Press Law Center, reported that in 1989 his organization had received hundreds of complaints. "Typically," Goodman said, "the censored articles involve criticism of school officials or policies or discussion of important social issues like drug abuse or AIDS."[19] Little wonder, therefore, that repressive policies at the national level by the executive, legislative, and judicial branches of government are not simply tolerated, but approved or ignored.

Weakening the Freedom of Information Act

Thus far, our coverage of secrecy and censorship issues at the national level during the Reagan-Bush era has dealt with the classification of government documents, lifetime nondisclosure agreements for government employees and contractors, mosaic or compilation theory (on which the FBI's Library Awareness Program was based), the Ethics Reform Act of 1989, the NEA controversies and much, much more.

No discussion of secrecy and censorship during the Reagan-Bush era would be complete, however, without an analysis of Samuel Loring Morison's conviction for espionage for leaking information to the press, the almost unrestricted power of the Office of Management and Budget to control the publication and dissemination of information essential for making enlightened public policy decisions, executive branch opposition to and efforts to manipulate international education and culture exchange programs, and efforts to restrict public access to government documents under the terms of the FOIA. The FOIA, enacted in 1966, and strengthened as a result of the Watergate revelations, has been an indispensable source in gaining access to information dealing with such questions as toxic wastes (Love Canal), nuclear safety, intelligence agency abuses, FBI abuses, hazards in the workplace, discrimination, civil rights violations, and consumer products safety. The Reagan administration did not succeed in destroying the FOIA (its original objective); but it managed to get modifications that deny public access to issues involving the use of nuclear energy (even peaceful uses— for example, nuclear power plant designs), information on consumer products (on the ground that its release might compromise trade secrets), and matters involving "national security"—including all operational files of the CIA and FBI records pertaining to foreign intelligence, counterintelligence operations, and international terrorism. Some safeguards in these areas are, in fact, necessary; but the past history of abuse demonstrates that the FBI and CIA want to impose the mantle of secrecy on all their activities, especially those illegal operations that have come to light.

Congressional concerns about restrictions on fee waivers led to the passage of legislation by Congress in 1986 designed to limit restrictions imposed by governmental agencies. Although commercial users were to be charged the full cost of locating and duplicating documents, fees charged to representatives of the news media, and of educational and scientific organizations, were limited to the actual costs of photoduplication itself. All other individuals or groups were required to pay for the first two hours of search time and the first one hundred pages of materials duplicated.

Unfortunately, this legislation, which was designed to facilitate access to government documents, had the opposite effect. The OMB issued new guidelines which interpreted the new legislation in ways that *limited* rather than *expanded* access to document categories that had not been restricted or eliminated by Congress earlier on. For example, the OMB guidelines not only ''gave agencies license to judge the value of the information requested,'' but some agencies began to reclassify some groups and individuals as commercial users. For example, the Pentagon classified the National Security Archive as a commercial user despite the fact that it is a non-profit research organization that provides information to the media. The NSA unsuccessfully sued the Pentagon. On July 28, 1989, the U.S. Court of Appeals, District of Columbia Circuit, ruled that the new fee waivers applied only to groups that ''gather information of potential interest to a segment of the public, *uses its editorial skills to turn the raw material into a distinct work, and distributes that work to an audience* [emphasis added].'' Clearly, the circuit court thwarted the legislative intent of the law.

Beyond this, government agencies also refused to apply the new rules governing access to information to the enormous amount of material stored electronically—arguing that such data did not constitute ''records'' within the meaning of the law. To date, the federal courts have consistently ruled that electronically stored material should be treated no differently than printed documents. But the costs of litigation are prohibitive in many instances; and one can only wonder just how many court cases will be required to force governmental agencies to provide such data without further litigation.

In sum: if the FOIA is not yet a "dead letter," the Reagan Administration not only succeeded in eliminating the availability of information in the categories mentioned above, but established roadblocks making it extremely difficult to gain access to information that is legally available—and this, despite the fact that Congress passed legislation in 1986 which, theoretically, was designed to facilitate access.[20]

The Enormous Power of the OMB

We have already observed that the powers of the OMB grew enormously during the Reagan years. It became the "nerve center" of the executive branch, a superagency that not only controls the budget but exercises an absolute veto power over the activities of all government regulatory agencies. The OMB also disregarded the intent of the Paperwork Reduction Act of 1980 by reducing, and in some cases eliminating, vital statistical information essential for informed public policy debates on the national, state, and local levels. In those instances where statistical information was not eliminated or reduced, its collection and dissemination have been farmed out to private contractors. Not only has the "commodification" of information greatly increased its cost, but, in the opinion of informed critics, has cast doubt in many instances upon its reliability or accuracy. "Paperwork reduction," as implemented by the Reagan administration became, therefore, another form of censorship.

In February 1990 the Supreme Court ruled in *Dole* v. *Steelworkers* that the OMB had overstepped its authority, under the terms of the Paperwork Reduction Act 1980, by disapproving an OSHA (Office of Occupational Safety and Health Administration) regulation which required "nearly all employers to warn their workers about the prospect of exposure to hazardous substances on the job." Unfortunately, the Court's ruling was far more limited in application than it appeared to be on first consideration. By confining its decision to the meaning of the Paperwork Reduction Act, the Court failed to address the OMB's regulatory powers under the terms of two executive orders issued by President Reagan. E.O. 12291, issued in 1981, "empowered the OMB to mold and supervise all the operations of the executive branch agencies." In late 1984 the

OMB's power over all regulatory agencies was strengthened even more by E.O. 12498 which, as Donna Demac observes, not only called for "a unified regulatory plan for the entire executive branch" but gave "the OMB director authority to review every regulatory activity 'planned or underway,' including the development of any documents that could lead to rule-making proceedings at a later date." In short, since *Dole* did not deal with the broader questions raised by Mr. Reagan's executive orders, the power of the OMB continues unabated.

The Leaker as "Spy": the Morison Case

Samuel Loring Morison, a strong advocate of a U.S. military buildup, is the first person ever convicted under the terms of the American espionage statutes for *leaking information to the press*. In the past, the espionage laws were directed primarily against persons who provided secret information to foreign enemies.[21] Morison, however, was convicted of espionage for providing a British magazine, *Jane's Defense Weekly*, with three classified photographs of the Soviet Union's first nuclear aircraft carrier.[22]

Joseph A. Young, the federal district judge who presided at Morison's trial, could have dismissed the charges against Morison by ruling that the espionage laws could not be used to prosecute leakers. Or, he might have instructed the jury that the prosecutors, in order to obtain a conviction, would have to prove, as required by the Espionage Act of 1917, that Morison intended to harm the United States by providing *Jane's* with photographs. Judge Young might also have said, in his charge to the jury, that the prosecutors also had to prove that the damage done to national security was "reasonably foreseeable, not remote or speculative." But Judge Young not only refused to dismiss the charges against Morison, but ruled that anyone who "willfully" transmits information is guilty of espionage "no matter what his motives." Young also ruled that the government did not have to prove that the photographs harmed national security. The transmission of classified information to unauthorized recipients, even if it had no effect on national security at all, was an act of espionage. Thus, Judge Young's interpretations of the espionage laws, however tortured, made Morison's conviction virtually a foregone conclusion since jurors must rely on a judge's rulings as to what laws mean.

But the issue involved here is not simply Judge Young's interpretations of the espionage laws. Morison's conviction was upheld by the United States Court of Appeals for the Fourth Circuit; and the Supreme Court, by refusing to hear his appeal, let his conviction stand. Technically, the Supreme Court's inaction meant that the Morison case did not create a national precedent. In fact, however, it has had a "chilling effect." The Reagan administration's goal of virtually eliminating all unauthorized leaks had been achieved by *judicial means* rather than *legislative enactment*. Stated in slightly different terms, the U.S. Congress has consistently refused to pass an American version of Great Britain's Official Secrets Act. This law, as Martin Garbus observes, "nearly gives the [British] government the final, judicially unreviewable right to impose its own definitions of what information injures the nation." The implications of the Morison case, therefore, are enormous. In the future, it is not only leakers who must beware, but journalists, broadcasters, authors, and publishers who receive such information and dare to use it. Even booksellers and magazine dealers can be prosecuted under the terms of *Morison*. As one commentator phrased it, the Reagan administration's information policies not only focused attention on security but equated "security with secrecy" and treated "information as if it were a potentially contagious disease that must be controlled, quarantined, and ultimately cured." The Reagan administration did not, and the Bush administration thus far has not used the enormous power at its disposal as a result of the Morison case. But the ability to do so has now become part of the institutionalized power structure of our "national security state."

Politicizing the USIA

Still another example of the Reagan administration's hostility to free inquiry and the open exchange of ideas is provided by its opposition to international educational and cultural exchanges.[23] In 1981 Charles Z. Wick, director of the United States Information Agency, recommended that funding for the Fulbright program be cut by 56 percent. This recommendation, had it been approved by Congress, would have eliminated Fulbright lectureships and research fellowships in sixty-one countries—primarily in Third World nations. In addition, Mr. Wick recommended that the Hubert H. Humphrey fellowship program be abolished and that drastic cuts be made in the critically important International Visitors Program. Fortunately, these funds were restored by a bipartisan coalition in Congress.

Besides this, the Reagan administration asked Congress each year, begining in 1981, to eliminate all funding under Title VI of the Higher Education Act. These proposed cuts would have eliminated funding for ninety-one international education and foreign language centers and for seventy-two undergraduate international studies programs at American colleges and universities. The administration's Title VI proposals would also have cut approximately $5 million each year for Fulbright graduate research fellowships. Conversely, the Reagan administration responded favorably to a Kissinger Commission report that recommended bringing some ten thousand Central American students to the United States to study at American universities at a cost of some $380 million. Congress has authorized funding for this initiative every year since 1986 but not at the levels requested.

The political and ideological motivations behind these contradictory initiatives are clear. As Latin-American historian Hugh M. Hamill, Jr. observes, the administration's efforts to weaken international education are predicated upon the idea that many U.S. educators and students "who do learn about Latin America and other areas of the world are articulate and effective critics" of American foreign policy. On the other hand, the administration apparently believed "that the Salvadorans, Hondurans and Guatemalans who study here will be so impressed by their experiences that they will return home to eschew possible revolutionary solutions to their problems and to inculcate North American values and institutions in place of Hispanic ones." If this was the case, then the administration's efforts were not merely short-sighted but self-defeating.

Equally disturbing was the USIA's politicization of its AMPARTS program—a program that sends some five hundred to six hundred speakers overseas each year. As early as 1983 the House Foreign Affairs Subcommittee on International Operations criticized USIA officials for "violating the letter and spirit of its charter." Not only had the USIA attempted to eliminate "educational and cultural affairs programs which have stood the test of time," but had chosen its AMPARTS speakers on the basis of "partisan political ideology."

It was not until early 1984, however, that USIA's policies became a national scandal. On January 31, the *Washington Post* revealed that since late 1981 the USIA had been compiling a blacklist. The list included the names of prominent academics and national figures including Coretta King, Representative Jack Brooks, and former Senator Gary Hart. Other administrations have sent speakers overseas to explain or defend some of their policies; but none has viewed USIA as an "American Propaganda Machine" (to use the *Hartford Courant's* phrase) whose sole function is to promote a particular president's foreign policy rather than present a balanced view of American life and society mandated by its charter.

THE RISE AND FALL OF THE AMERICAN UMPIRE

Paul Conrad. Copyright, 1991, Los Angeles Times.
Reprinted with permission.

The FBI:
"Police State" Tactics

The Reagan administration's search for "total security" was not a piecemeal process. It extended to nearly every aspect of American life. Each policy initiative formed part of a carefully crafted mosaic or tapestry that blended together to form part of a unified whole. It came as no surprise, therefore, that the administration authorized the resumption of "open-ended" domestic security investigations by the FBI. The FBI has a legitimate role to play by investigating organized crime and other groups who use force or violence in efforts to achieve social and political ends; but beginning in 1981, the FBI's investigations included individuals or groups whose only "crime" was their outspoken opposition to President Reagan's foreign policy.

The FBI Under Hoover

Before analyzing the Reagan administration's policies, it needs to be emphasized that the history of the FBI's domestic security investigations has been characterized by illegality and abuse. For example, the FBI, during the Red Scare of the 1920s, kept secret files on approximately two hundred thousand Americans. Moreover, former FBI Director J. Edgar Hoover, without authorization from Congress or any president, launched a highly secret operation called COINTELPRO in 1957. Between that year and 1974 the FBI kept files on the activities of nearly five hundred thousand Americans whom Hoover and other FBI officials considered to be "subversives" or potential "national security risks."

The FBI's repertoire of illegal activities included break-ins, bugging, wire-tapping, mail-tampering, character defamation, and the use of paid informants or undercover agents to infiltrate "subversive" organizations. Among the organizations infiltrated were the

NAACP, the Socialist Workers Party, the Medical Committee for Human Rights, the National Lawyers Guild, and even a Milwaukee Boy Scout troop.

These activities came to light as a result of the Watergate revelations, congressional hearings (most notably, the Church committee's detailed investigations), and information obtained under FOIA requests. As a result, Attorney General Edward Levi in April 1976 promulgated for the first time "a set of public guidelines governing the initiation and scope of the FBI domestic security investigations."[24]

The Levi Guidelines

The Levi guidelines, by establishing a criminal standard for investigations, eliminated FBI surveillance of dissident political groups. They authorized full domestic security investigations only "on the basis of *specific and articulable facts* [emphasis added] giving reason to believe that an individual or group is or may be engaged in [unlawful] activities which involve the use of force or violence." Beyond this, the FBI was instructed to take into consideration the "magnitude of the threatened harm," "the likelihood that it will occur," the "immediacy of the threat," and the "danger to privacy and free expression posed by a full investigation."[25]

The Levi guidelines had a dramatic impact. In March 1976 the FBI was conducting 4,868 domestic security investigations. By December 1981 the number had dropped to only 26 and the organizations being investigated, such as the Jewish Defense League, the Communist Workers Party, and the Arizona chapter of the Ku Klux Klan, were apparently involved in violent criminal activity.

The Smith Guidelines Replace Levi's

The Reagan administration eliminated the safeguards against FBI abuse that the Levi guidelines were designed to prevent. It did so by promulgating two interrelated executive branch initiatives: Executive Order 12333, which was issued in 1981, and Attorney General William French Smith's guidelines, which replaced Levi's in 1983.

The Smith guidelines eliminated the "probable cause" standard contained in the "specific and articulable facts" requirement of the Levi guidelines. They state that the FBI can launch domestic security investigations if the facts "reasonably indicate" that groups or individuals are involved in criminal activity. Moreover, the Smith guidelines apply the "enterprise concept," which has been used in organized crime investigations, to domestic security cases. This permits the FBI to investigate the activities of groups and individuals who "knowingly support" terrorist or subversive groups but do not themselves engage in violence. Such an application, argues Geoffrey Stone, Dean of the University of Chicago Law School, was totally inappropriate.[26] More important, the new guidelines also authorized the FBI to "anticipate or prevent crime." As a result, the FBI is now permitted to investigate groups or individuals whose statements "advocate criminal activity or *indicate an apparent intent to engage in crime, particularly crimes of violence*" [emphasis added].[27]

The Smith guidelines, which are still in force, are clearly far more permissive than Levi's. The terminology of the guidelines is specific in some instances but deliberately vague in others. In short, the language provides FBI officials with sufficient interpretive latitude to investigate virtually any group or individual they choose to target, including political activists opposed to the Reagan or Bush administration's foreign policy.

The most permissive aspect of the Smith guidelines, perhaps, is the authorization of domestic security investigations against individuals or groups whose statements "indicate an apparent intent to engage in crime." It assumes that the abstract advocacy of violence, even though it is not accompanied by violence itself, provides sufficient grounds for investigation. This position flies in the face of the Supreme Court's decision in *Brandenburg* v. *Ohio* (1969), which draws a sharp distinction between expression and *conduct*. In *Brandenburg*, the Court ruled that speech is protected except where advocacy of law violation is "directed to inciting or producing imminent lawless action and is likely to incite or produce such action." The Court thus took the position that the premises behind abstract advocacy may contain radical criticisms of government or society that deserve a hearing.

The *Brandenburg* standard, however, has come under attack in the courts. Circuit court Judge Richard Posner, a Reagan appointee, wrote a majority opinion in *Alliance to End Repression* v. *Chicago* which declared that although *Brandenburg* protects proponents of abstract advocacy from criminal prosecution, it does not rule out domestic security investigations if they are "properly motivated."

However, the problem with many past FBI investigations, Professor Stone observes, "was not that they were improperly motivated, but that they were the product of exaggerated fears, bad judgment, and insensitivity to the value of constitutional rights."[28]

Reagan's Executive Order 12333

The terms of President Reagan's Executive Order 12333, which deals with the permissible activities of the intelligence agencies, are equally reactionary. This order, like other Reagan edicts is, to repeat for emphasis, still being enforced. The order states that the CIA and the other intelligence agencies are authorized to conduct "counterintelligence" activities within the United States so long as they are coordinated with the FBI. It also states that the FBI, when requested.by the CIA or another intelligence agency, "can collect foreign intelligence information or support foreign intelligence collection requirements." An earlier draft of the executive order authorized the CIA to directly infiltrate and influence domestic organizations without a warrant. But the terms of the CIA's charter, issued in 1947, specifically prohibit such activity. Thus, the terminology of the final order is little more than a subterfuge. Its wording may comply with the letter of CIA's charter, but clearly not its spirit.

On the surface, the order appears to provide some safeguards against abuse. It states that "no foreign intelligence by such agencies may be taken for the purpose of acquiring information concerning the domestic activities of United States persons." But, as historian Athan Theoharis and law professor Diana M.T.K. Autin both observe, this prohibition was an inadequate safeguard at best.[29] The fact is that President Reagan and other administration spokesmen argued that the domestic activities of dissident groups such as the Sojourners, the Sanctuary movement, Quest for Peace, the anti-nuclear movement, and CISPES (Committee in Solidarity with the People of El Salvador) were infiltrated and influenced by foreign agents. As Theoharis phrases it, "Reagan's executive order, in effect, authorized the FBI to resume investigating [the] dissident political activities" of American citizens.[30]

Until late January 1988, the scale on which such investigations were occurring could not be ascertained; but sufficient evidence had surfaced by the mid 1980s to show beyond question that numerous investigations of groups and individuals were underway. According to congressional sources, the FBI, in 1985 alone, conducted ninety-six investigations of groups and individuals opposed to the Reagan administrations' Central American policies. Furthermore, Frank Varelli, a former FBI informant, testified before a congressional subcommittee that between 1981 and 1984 he succeeded in infiltrating the Dallas chapter of CISPES. During that time he provided the FBI with 3,500 pages of information regarding the activities of CISPES members. In an interview with CBS *Evening News*, Varelli stated that FBI officials instructed him to "find the guns." When Varelli reported that CISPES had no weapons, he was instructed to continue his search until he found them. Furthermore, the FBI admitted to the *National Catholic Reporter* that it was keeping files on Seattle Archbishop Raymond Hunthausen, an activist involved in the antinuclear movement, and on Detroit's Auxiliary Bishop Thomas Gumbleton, the spokesperson for Quest for Peace, an organization that provides humanitarian aid to Nicaragua in the form of food, clothing and medical supplies.

Then, in late January 1988 the Center for Constitutional Rights in New York released information obtained from the FBI under FOIA requests revealing that in addition to CISPES, the Sanctuary movement, Quest for Peace, and antinuclear groups, the FBI had also targeted the Southern Leadership Conference, the Maryknoll Sisters in Chicago, the American Federation of Teachers, and the United Auto Workers in Cleveland. Moreover, another document obtained by the CCR revealed that an FBI agent in Philadelphia provided FBI headquarters in Washington with the names of another dozen groups "actively involved in demonstrations, seminars, marches, *et cetera*, regarding U.S. intervention in Central America." In fact, all of the FBI's fifty-nine regional offices were involved in open ended domestic security investigations.

On January 29, White House spokesperson, Marlin Fitzwater, stated that President Reagan had ordered an internal review of FBI surveillance activities because the president was opposed to "investigations of Americans for their political beliefs." Fitzwater went on to say that "no one in the White House or the National Security Council knew about the five-year surveillance campaign." The responsibility, according to Fitzwater, rested entirely with former FBI Director William Webster.[31]

Paul Conrad. Copyright, 1989, Los Angeles Times.
Reprinted with permission.

On February 3, however, the White House changed its position. Mr. Reagan, Fitzwater stated, had accepted current FBI Director Sessions' explanation that the FBI was not involved in "massive" surveillance of groups and individuals opposed to the Administration's Central American policies. Its investigations, Sessions maintained, were confined primarily to CISPES. This investigation, Fitzwater continued, was based on allegations that CISPES had links to leftist rebels in El Salvador who were carrying out terrorist acts. The investigation ended in 1985, Fitzwater maintained, "after investigators determined that CISPES was a legitimate political group."[32]

These White House contradictions were neither surprising nor convincing. The evidence of FBI abuse that has surfaced since the early 1980s appears to be irrefutable. Moreover, in light of the permissive terminology contained in President Reagan's Executive Order 12333 and the replacement of the Levi guidelines by Attorney General William French Smith's in 1983, open-ended domestic security investigations are perfectly legal. In sum, the very activities that were illegal during J. Edgar Hoover's heyday have been legitimized by executive branch fiat![33]

Equally alarming: President Reagan's E.O. 12333 is extremely permissive in permitting the FBI to use warrantless wiretaps. Some critics of the Reagan administration, who have found many provisions of the executive order odious, have denied that it permits unrestricted electronic surveillance of American citizens; but the terms of the executive order are unmistakably clear. In its "counterintelligence" operations, the FBI is permitted to utilize intrusive techniques that otherwise would be illegal—for example, mail and physical surveillance, theft, unconsented physical searches, and the use of infiltrators and informants. And, as Diana M.T.K. Autin observes, the executive order permits the use of warrantless wiretaps if *"the Attorney General has determined in each case that there is probable cause to believe that the technique is directed against a foreign power or an agent of a foreign power"* [emphasis added].[34] An earlier draft of the executive order actually contained a provision stating that the "inherent powers" of the presidency permitted the use of warrantless wiretaps in "national security" cases. This provision was deleted after objections were raised by members of the congressional intelligence committees who reviewed it. Even so, the order provided Attorney Generals William French Smith, Edwin Meese and, indeed, Dick Thornburgh and William Barr with carte blanche.

THROUGH THE LOOKING GLASS

Paul Conrad. Copyright, 1988, Los Angeles Times.
Reprinted with permission.

THOUGHT CONTROL AND REPRESSION

Since the FBI's use of other intrusive techniques to monitor the activities of political dissidents is undeniable, the use of warrantless wiretaps by the Reagan and Bush administrations appears to be not only likely, but probable.

Nothing Changes Under Bush

During the Bush era, despite public relations efforts by the White House and current FBI Director Sessions to portray the agency's activities in a more benign light, the FBI continues to monitor the legitimate political activities of American citizens. During the Gulf War, for example, the FBI investigated the activities and opinions of scores of Arab-Americans—utilizing an "anti-terrorist" rationale to justify its actions. Moreover, the Government Accounting Office issued a report at the request of Representative Don Edwards, which revealed that between 1982 and 1988, the FBI had conducted nearly 19,000 investigations of American citizens, resident aliens, and foreign students in a fruitless effort to discover links to international terrorist organizations. Not to be outdone, the CIA also got into the act.[35]

In October 1990, at the University of Connecticut, for example, a man named Daniel Alhimook, who identified himself as a CIA agent approached Richard Vengroth, Dean of International Affairs. Alhimook asked Vengroth to provide him with a list that included the names of all foreign students enrolled at the university, their areas of academic concentration, the names of their advisers, and their countries of origin. Vengroth refused to comply and informed an astonished Alhimook that the only thing he was entitled to was a student directory which was available to anyone who cared to use it. Vengroth further informed Alhimook that his request was not only unethical but in all probability illegal. CIA headquarters in Langley, Virginia, in response to a phone call from a *Hartford Courant* reporter, refused to "confirm or deny" Alhimook's mission or even his existence. When Alhimook died in 1992, his obituary stated only that he was a long-time government employee.[36]

The Campaign Against Earth First!

As we have seen, the FBI's obsession with "national security," and its surveillance and harassment of political dissidents, has produced a number of bizarre turns and twists. It has been duly noted that the FBI has a number of legitimate functions to perform including investigations of organized crime and organizations such as the Jewish Defense League (now the Jewish Defense Organization), the Arizona chapter of the KKK, and the Communist Workers Party that have utilized violence in pursuing their objectives. But most groups, perceived by the FBI to be comprised of dangerous revolutionaries or radicals, hardly deserve to be characterized in this way. Consider, for example, the FBI's investigations, infiltration, and harassment of a loosely organized group of environmentalists called Earth First!

In Oakland, California, Earth First! activists Darryl Cherney and Judy Barry organized a campaign called Redwood Summer which opposed the plans of lumbering interests to cut old-growth forests in northern California. Although the couple had not engaged in violence of any kind, they received numerous death threats. In May 1990, the car in which they were riding was severely damaged by a mysterious explosion. Cherney and Barry were immediately charged by the Oakland police for carrying the bomb themselves with the intent of using it in violent protest against logging practices. The police also raided the home of a group of local environmental activists without a warrant.

Although the state's attorney declined to prosecute Cherney or Barry, FBI officials falsely implied that they had the evidence to do so—thus creating a climate of hostility and suspicion against Earth First! "Even now," writes investigative reporter Chip Berlet, "the FBI has yet to follow up on several obvious clues on who planted the bomb, [and] the death threats received by the pair in the months before the bombing."[37]

In Arizona, however, the FBI not only succeeded in infiltrating another Earth First! group but federal prosecutors managed to convince a grand jury to indict Dave Foreman, a co-founder of Earth First! and four other activists who became known as the "Arizona Five." These Earth First! activists, reportedly, engaged in "monkeywrenching" whereby they spiked old-growth trees to prevent them from being harvested, disabled bulldozers by putting sugar in their gas tanks, and committed other acts of vandalism in the name of environmentalism. But acts of "monkeywrenching" were not the alleged crimes for which the Arizona Five were indicted. They were charged with the crime of conspiracy for allegedly planning to blow up power lines connected to a nuclear plant.

"You will learn," federal prosecutor Roslyn Moore-Silver thundered, "that this case is about *anarchy and revolution* [emphasis added]." Prosecutors portrayed the Arizona Five as a gang of "malicious terrorists willing to risk a nuclear meltdown to further their credo 'No compromise in defense of Mother Earth.' "[38]

In the end, the case was not about anarchy and revolution at all, but about the credibility of the FBI, federal prosecutors, and FBI informant, Ronald Frazier, a former member of Earth First! who, after being jilted by his lover, agreed to become an informant for $50,000. The government paid the money in cash to enable Frazier to avoid an IRS lien on his earnings!

The trial of the Arizona Five, which began in 1991, rapidly degenerated into a farce (or perhaps a black comedy) after Frazier, the FBI's star witness, informed the prosecutors that he had a major drug problem. Frazier, as reporter Bill McKibben phrased it, was "a one man Rexall." The revelation, McKibben continued,

left the government in the interesting position of explaining to the jury why his intake of marijuana, peyote, psilocybin, amphetamines, barbiturates, heroin, and LSD had not hampered his ability to perceive or remember events.[39]

But the prosecutors tried. During the period of Frazier's heaviest use of LSD, the prosecutors explained, he did college-level honors work on diesel technology and won second prize "in some statewide mechanics competition." In addition, the FBI flew Frazier to San Antonio, Texas for sessions with a psychologist who supposedly taught a "glassy-eyed" Frazier to "bridge in" and "bridge out" of a trance. These sessions were designed to enable Frazier to recall "peripheral" conversations with Earth First! members. Lo and behold, it worked! Frazier recalled a conversation during which someone talked about disabling a steam locomotive. Since steam locomotives were no longer in existence, this was "great stuff" McKibben explained—testimony about "Earth First! circa 1875."[40]

Little wonder, therefore, that federal prosecutors dropped conspiracy charges to "risk a nuclear meltdown" in return for plea bargains—the most serious of which involved disabling a ski-lift. Thus, the trial of the Arizona Five came to an inglorious end. The entire process had consumed two years' time, had involved the services of approximately 100 FBI agents at one time or another, and had cost the taxpayers over $3 million.

Mr. Bush once declared that he wanted to become known as the "environmental president." Would that this were true, and that the executive, legislative, and judicial branches of government would exhibit as much zeal in protecting the environment as the FBI does in investigating, harassing, and prosecuting Earth First! members accused of "monkeywrenching." But then, zeal alone is not enough. Zeal, to be socially useful, requires good judgment and sensitivity to the value of constitutional rights.

H.R. 50: "The FBI First Amendment Protection Act."

As we observed earlier on, Attorney General Levi's guidelines temporarily eliminated open-ended domestic security investigations by the FBI. By requiring strict adherence to a probable cause standard, the number of such investigations declined from 4,868 in March 1976 to only 26 in December 1981. But President Reagan's Executive Order 12333 and the Smith guidelines, which replaced Levi's, once again unleashed the FBI. The number of FBI domestic security investigations increased from only 26 in 1982 to more than 19,000 between 1982 and 1988—a grim reminder of the extent to which the FBI, once again, has careened out of control. "The greatest dangers to liberty," Justice Louis Brandeis once observed, "lurk in insidious encroachment by men of zeal, well meaning, but without understanding."

During the early 1980s efforts to secure passage of a law creating an FBI charter failed—in part because the proposed charter legislation, as amended, was so reactionary that moderate and liberal members of Congress managed to defeat it. As a result, the FBI continues to be "regulated" by the Smith guidelines and by President Reagan's Executive Order 12333 which also "monitors" the activities of the CIA and the other intelligence agencies.

New efforts to minimize and eventually eliminate FBI abuses are now underway. H.R. 50: "The FBI First Amendment Protection Act," introduced by Rep. Don Edwards (D-CA) and Rep. John Conyers (D-MI), H.R. 50 would

- Prohibit FBI investigations of First Amendment-related activity (including political work) where there is no evidence of criminal acts.

- Prohibit FBI investigations of organizations engaged in First Amendment protected activities without evidence that most of the members are engaged in criminal activity.

- Allow victims of FBI political spying and other invasions of their First Amendment activity to sue the FBI for monetary damages.

- Place stringent limits on the extent of political and personal information the FBI may collect during a criminal investigation.

The National Committee Against Repressive Legislation (NCARL), among other organizations, is in the forefront of the battle to secure passage of H.R. 50; but the final outcome is far from clear.[41]

The New Right's
Judicial Philosophy

The Reagan-Bush Constitutional Agenda

President Reagan's impact on the federal judiciary, which has been extended and consolidated by President Bush, promises to become his most enduring legacy. Mr. Reagan's elevation of William Rehnquist to Chief Justice, his appointments of Sandra Day O'Connor, Antonin Scalia, and Anthony Kennedy to the Supreme Court, in combination with Mr. Bush's appointment of Justices David Souter and Clarence Thomas to the High Court, assures the ascendancy of a "conservative" majority that is now in process of revolutionizing constitutional law—a revolution that will last well into the twenty first century if current policies provide an accurate prognosis.

President Bush is far less concerned with domestic than with foreign policy issues, and, arguably, is more concerned with the exercise of power for its own sake than principle. But whether or not President Bush is, in fact, a conservative ideologue or a political opportunist makes very little difference in terms of practical effects. As we have observed, Mr. Bush's policies reveal him to be a "codifier" rather than an "innovator," and the priorities of the Reagan Revolution, for whatever reasons, have become his own.

Less dramatic than Supreme Court appointments, but equally important, is the fact that Mr. Reagan, by the end of his presidency, had appointed nearly half of the nation's seven hundred forty-four federal judges. By the end of 1992, the combined number appointed by both presidents Reagan and Bush will reach approximately seventy percent.

During his presidency, Mr. Reagan gladly appointed qualified conservative ideologues to the federal bench when they were available—for example, Richard Posner, Ralph Winter, Antonin Scalia, and Robert Bork. However, it was not professional competence but ideological purity that was the Reagan administration's primary criterion in selecting judges.

It may be objected that the nature of Mr. Reagan's appointments did not differ drastically from that of other presidents. Presidents, after all, ordinarily prefer judges whose ideology is compatible with their own. Although this argument carries some weight, there was a "qualitative difference" that characterized President Reagan's choice of judges. In the past, writes Jamie Kalven, a specialist on constitutional law, judicial selection processes have had the "saving grace of messiness"—that is, court appointments reflected diversity in terms of values and interests represented. Mr. Reagan's selection process, by contrast was "unprecedented in its unwavering clarity of purpose, its narrowly ideological criteria, and its single-minded diligence."[42] As the number of judicial appointments mounted, therefore, the professional competence of individuals elevated to the federal bench began to decline.

Equally important, Mr. Bush appointed a screening committee early in his presidency that continues to apply an ideological litmus test to all prospective appointees to the federal bench. In sum, during the Reagan-Bush era, the executive branch has relentlessly pursued its objective of creating a federal judiciary dominated by judges committed to the New Right's constitutional agenda.

What is that agenda? Among other things, it includes restricting or eliminating procedural protections for criminal defendants, the elimination of affirmative action, the reversal of *Roe* v. *Wade*, restricting the right to privacy in a variety of other contexts, placing limits on First Amendment principles, and the advocacy of a more relaxed standard in matters involving the separation of church and state.

If the courts made a number of retrograde decisions prior to 1989, the year 1989 marks the beginning of a systematic assault by the Supreme Court, which promises to transfer the Reagan Administration's constitutional "wish list" from a state of advocacy to the realm of harsh reality. The vote of Justice Souter, Mr. Bush's appointee, made the difference, more often than not, in a series of closely contested decisions. Justice Thomas's appointment may encourage the now dominant conservative majority to make even more sweeping pronouncements than it was inclined to do on the basis of 5-4 rulings. Before proceeding to an analysis of specific cases which illustrate the wide-ranging process of constitutional "demolition," it is essential to analyze the implications of some of the major principles that characterize the New Right's judicial philosophy.

The doctrine of "judicial restraint"—a demand that judges base their opinions on the "original intent" of the Framers rather than their own subjective value judgments—occupies center stage in the theories expounded by former Attorney General Edwin Meese, Chief Justice Rehnquist, Justice Scalia, Judge Robert Bork and other neo-conservative theorists.

However plausible or appealing the doctrine of "original intent" may appear on the surface, it overlooks a number of critically important factors. For one thing, the Constitution of the United States was not etched in stone. "The Framers," as Professor Leonard Levy observes, "had a genius for studied imprecision. They were conscious of the need to phrase the constitution in generalized terms and without a lexicographical guide, for they meant to outline an instrument that would serve future generations."

Equally important, the Constitution also contained important contradictions—contradictions that could not be resolved by legal theorizing, but only by the process of historical experience. For example, only historical experience could resolve the contradictory implications inherent in the elastic clause and the Tenth Amendment. The theory of "strict construction" was based on the phraseology of the Tenth Amendment, which states that powers not expressly granted to the central government by the Constitution were reserved to the states. Conversely the "elastic clause," in Article I, Section 8 of the U.S. Constitution, justified a "loose constructionist" interpretation that would strengthen the power of the central government by permitting it to do anything not specifically prohibited by the Constitution so long as it was necessary and proper to promote the general welfare.

Moreover, it was not the original text of the Constitution that empowered the Supreme Court to declare laws passed by Congress unconstitutional. It was, rather, *Marbury* v. *Madison* (1803), which not only established the doctrine of judicial review over congressional legislation but, arguably, preserved the Union itself by creating a mechanism which gave the Supreme Court the "last word" in resolving legal and constitutional disputes. The passage of the Alien and Sedition Acts in 1798 by a Federalist-dominated Congress was countered by the Democratic-Republicans, led by Madison and Jefferson, with the doctrine of nullification contained in the Virginia and Kentucky Resolutions. In sum, *Marbury* saved the day. As Anthony Lewis so aptly phrases it, the doctrine of "original intention" is little more than "a historical theory, with no basis in history."

Historical accuracy, however, is not the intent of such theoretical formulations. Their intentions, rather, are ideological in nature—examples of sophistry designed to buttress their vision, not merely of the Constitution, but the type of society the New Right would like to inhabit and is, in fact, in process of creating. The views expressed by Chief Justice Rehnquist on the separation of powers, state autonomy, due process, individual rights, and majority rule illustrate the point.[43]

Chief Justice Rehnquist: No Longer the Supreme Court's "Lone Ranger"

Mr. Rehnquist argues that "the primary responsibility of the Supreme Court is not merely the preservation of state autonomy against incursions by the federal government, but to protect the states from challenges by individuals claiming that state laws or arbitrary decisions by state courts have violated their constitutional rights." Mr. Rehnquist's views on the separation of powers, thus require him to argue that the doctrine of incorporation has limited applicability despite the fact that the Supreme Court, since the 1920s, has extended the Bill of Rights to include the states.

In *Dandridge* v. *Williams* (1970), for example, Rehnquist's dissenting opinion maintained that the Bill of Rights prevents states from encroaching on individual rights only when state action is "irrational." Two years later, in *Furman* v. *Georgia*, Rehnquist's dissent declared that it is "far worse to hold a [state] statute unconstitutional than to deny an individual his/her civil rights." In short, Rehnquist would permit the states to restrict freedom of speech or press in ways that would "violate the First Amendment if done by the federal government." He argued that the Fourteenth Amendment's equal protection clause applies to the states only on racial issues, and "only then when segregation was the explicit policy of the state."

Rehnquist thereby rejects an organic view of constitutional development. In a *Texas Law Review* article, "The Notion of a Living Constitution," published in 1976, Rehnquist in reiterating the doctrine of "original intent," argued that the concept of the "living Constitution, is an end run around popular government . . . and is generally *corrosive of the fundamental values of our democratic society"* [emphasis added]. Those "who wish to protect new rights," Rehnquist declared on another occasion, "such as those of women, the right to an abortion, or the rights of aliens or prisoners should look to the legislatures or the constitutional amendment process rather than to existing constitutional principles as applied by the Courts to new conditions."

In the 1970s Justice Rehnquist was sometimes referred to as the Supreme Court's "Lone Ranger." In 1991 his views are far from being singular. It is one of the ironies of history, perhaps, that Rehnquist and other conservative ideologues would use massive applications of judicial power to downgrade the role of the federal judiciary in American society which, in turn would promote an unparalleled exercise of power by the executive and legislative branches of government. Their *notion* of "popular government," therefore, would eliminate the traditional system of checks and balances that have been an integral part of the American constitutional system since the 1790s; and they would do so precisely because New Right ideologues consider many of the Supreme Court's past decisions intolerable. If their views are cast "in the idiom of conservatism," theirs, as Jamie Kalven observes, is actually a "radical vision" that subverts fundamental constitutional principles established over time, including the doctrine of incorporation.

Whether liberals, conservatives, moderates, or reactionaries like it or not, or want to admit it, the Constitution of the United States, at any given point in time, is precisely what the Supreme Court says that it is. Little wonder, therefore, that Justice Marshall, dissenting in *Payne* v. *Tennessee* (1991), declared: "Power, not reason, is the currency of this Court's decision making." This brief analysis, drawn primarily from a 1986 ACLU report on Mr. Rehnquist's judicial philosophy, is far from comprehensive; but it does provide insight into some of the fundamental principles on which his jurisprudence, and indeed, his social vision is based.

Judge Bork's First Amendment Theories

If the implications of Chief Justice Rehnquist's judicial philosophy ought to give pause to all Americans who value individual rights, another case in point is that of Judge Robert Bork whose views on the right of free expression are so cramped and limited that they would rob the First Amendment of most of its meaning.

Bork's failed nomination to the Supreme court was, at best, a hollow victory for civil libertarians. As with Justice Rehnquist and the other Supreme Court conservatives, Judge Bork's ideology is a simple majoritarianism. He would give state and federal lawmaking bodies wide latitude in making laws regulating whole new areas of public and private activities. Political, economic, racial and gender minorities whose views and interests are not respected in the prevailing political atmosphere, he argued in *The Tempting of America,* should no longer be able to turn to the courts for redress as they did in the Warren era. Rather, they should seek remedies in the political arena. For Bork, the "tyranny of the majority," which Alexis de Tocqueville warned of in the 1830's, is a *modus operandi.*

In order to put his views into practical action, Bork's judicial philosophy dictates that the courts play an extremely limited role in reviewing state and federal legislation. This is particularly disturbing in the area of First Amendment issues. For example, in a 1971 law review article, Judge Bork contended:

> Constitutional protection should be extended only to speech that is explicitly political. There is no basis for judicial intervention to protect any other form of expression, be it scientific, literary or that variety of expression we call obscene or pornographic. Moreover, within that category of speech we ordinarily call political, there should be no constitutional obstruction to laws making criminal any speech that advocates forcible overthrow of the government or the violation of any law.

Among other things, Bork's view implies that if political majorities wish to restrict a whole set of minority ideas, the courts would be remiss in preventing it. This rather simplistic conception of democracy completely ignores the nearly insurmountable difficulties that minorities of various kinds have in obtaining justice and representation in a hostile political environment.

Underlying Bork's views is a confidence that majorities in the several states will be able to enact the conservative vision of society that he and the other members of the New Right movement hold so dear. The frustration which he and others of his ideological persuasion felt in the Warren era is quite evident from their published works and judicial decisions. As the New Right definition of the good society is ultimately hostile to the rights of minorities, their judicial philosophy is an attempt to keep the court system from preserving its twentieth-century role as guarantor of those fundamental freedoms.

As Jamie Kalven phrases it, Judge Bork's views reflect "a bizarre divorce of political discourse from its social and cultural foundations." Moreover, Bork contends that "political truth" is what "the majority thinks it is at any given moment." Finally, Bork argues that "subversive advocacy" (another phrase for the theoretical "right of revolution") has no value "within a republican system of government." In fact, as we have already noted, the Supreme Court has ruled, most recently in *Brandenburg* v. *Ohio*, that speech is protected "except where advocacy of law violation is directed to inciting or producing imminent lawless action and is likely to incite or produce such action."

If one carries Judge Bork's views to their logical conclusion, it appears that the theoretical foundations on which the American Revolution was based are illegitimate, as are the moral postulates that led Henry David Thoreau and Martin Luther King to advocate civil disobedience. In sum, Mr. Bork's views can only lead, as Justice Brandeis phrased it, to "silence coerced by law."

Judge Bork, responding to an article written by Kalven, maintained that his views on protected speech have been broadened to include "many other forms of discourse" such as "moral and scientific debate." Even so, Bork's reply said nothing about artistic expression (including literature, art, and film) which, arguably, would leave the door open to attacks on "obscenity" and "pornography." More important, Bork made no mention whatever of his views on abstract advocacy even though most of Kalven's analysis of Bork's intellectual universe focused on this issue.

Judge Bork's testimony on *Brandenburg* during his confirmation hearings was contradictory at best. At one point, Bork stated that the Court's decision in *Brandenburg* "is okay. That is a good test." Later on, he told Senator Specter: "[o]n *Brandenburg*, I did not say my mind had changed. . . . I think *Brandenburg* may have gone too far—went too far, but I accept it as a judge and I have no desire to overturn it. . . . It's settled law. That's all I've said. I haven't said these writings [that is, his earlier criticisms of *Brandenburg*] were wrong."

But even if one accepts Bork's view that he now accepts *Brandenburg* as "settled law," Burke Marshall, a Yale law professor, testified that a judge could "accept" precedents "while variously restricting the application of such precedents to their original facts.'' In short, new cases always deal with new facts involving a change of time, place, and circumstances. A judge, therefore, could reach different conclusions than those contained in *Brandenburg*. In the end, Judge Bork's changing positions led the Senate Judiciary Committee to conclude that "He Might Not Fully Apply This Vital Precedent.''

If Bork's views on abstract advocacy have not changed, and there is little basis for thinking otherwise, they are by no means singular. As Geoffrey Stone observes, Circuit Court Judge Richard Posner's decision in the *Alliance* case took exception to part of the Supreme Court's ruling in *Brandenburg*. Moreover, Judge Joseph A. Young's decision in the *Morison* case ignored the legislative intent of the espionage statutes. Its framers clearly had no intention of applying it to "leakers." Judge Young also ignored the act's provision requiring federal prosecutors to prove an intent to harm the United States in order to obtain a conviction. Moreover, the opinions by Justices Rehnquist, Scalia, and O'Connor in *U.S.* v. *Salerno* hardly reflect a commitment to the concept of individual rights. The conclusion is inescapable, therefore, that the call for ''judicial restraint'' is not so much a principled philosophical position as it is a *weapon to be used or ignored* in promoting conservative political objectives.

The Supreme Court
v. the Bill of Rights

The New Majority Takes Control

The fact that the year 1989 represents a major turning point in American judicial history obviously does not mean that the Supreme Court's record before that fateful year was always enlightened. We have already noted, for example, that whereas the Supreme Court, at the height of the Cold War, did not launch a major assault on First Amendment principles, it often ignored them. Moreover, the Court's decision in *U.S.* v. *Salerno* (1987) upheld the constitutionality of preventive detention which was not simply an act of constitutional "demolition," but a decision that reflects the mentality encountered in a "police state."

Even so, the constitutional agenda of President Reagan, Chief Justice Rehnquist, Judge Bork, Justice Scalia and other conservative ideologues and advocates, could not be fully implemented until the New Right had achieved a majority on the court. Mr. Bush's appointment of Justice Souter in 1989 finally accomplished that goal, and Justice Thomas's confirmation by the Senate in 1991 consolidated the New Majority's power. Beginning in 1989, therefore, the New Majority launched a counterrevolution in American constitutional law. Although "the Reagan Revolution," in judicial terms, is still in its early stages, the Supreme Court has profoundly altered the world in which we live in only three years time. In the sections that follow, our analysis will concentrate on abortion, First Amendment issues, civil rights (especially affirmative action), and restrictions on the procedural rights of convicted criminals—especially efforts to undermine and eventually eliminate the writ of *habeas corpus*. We will also analyze the reversal of important precedents that protected the rights of convicted felons and criminal defendants

Paul Conrad. Copyright, 1986, Los Angeles Times.
Reprinted with permission.

on substantive questions—e.g. coerced confessions and victim impact testimony at the time of sentencing. In addition, we will consider drug testing cases and the watering down of the probable cause standard in drug cases.

Considering the number and complexity of the issues and cases involved, our analysis here, of necessity, must be suggestive rather than comprehensive. If breadth has its limitations, it can also provide a panoramic view of the forest as well as some of the trees.

First Amendment and Abortion Cases

Ordinarily, First Amendment and abortion cases would be analyzed separately. But in *Webster* v. *Reproductive Health Services* (1989) and *Rust* v. *Sullivan* (1991), the issues of abortion and freedom of expression are inextricably joined. In *Webster*, the Court upheld the constitutionality of Missouri's law prohibiting the expenditure of public funds for the purpose of "encouraging or counselling a woman to have an abortion not necessary to save her life." Fearful of the law's implications, the American Library Association filed an *amicus* brief. Although the law's application had been restricted to hospitals and clinics, the ALA asked the Court to consider the impact of the law on intellectual freedom—especially the dissemination by libraries of information about abortion, contraception, or other aspects of sexuality. Justice O'Connor declared that such questions would have to be decided by Missouri's Supreme Court on a case-by-case basis; but Chief Justice Rehnquist disagreed. Rehnquist, as Justice Blackmun phrased it, gave "winks, nods, and knowing glances" to state legislators who not only wanted to restrict access to abortion but to information on various aspects of sexuality including birth control. The legislators could cut off funding to any public agency, he said, by declaring that the dissemination of such information was "contrary to the public interest." According to Rehnquist, therefore, First Amendment issues were not even involved! The state would only be making a "value judgment" or "policy choice" in deciding how to allocate funds.

If *Webster* was characterized by disagreements, Rehnquist's reasoning carried the day in *Rust* v. *Sullivan* (1991). In this case, the Court's majority ruled that guidelines for federally-funded family planning clinics, which prohibited clinic personnel from providing counselling or information on abortion, were constitutional. *Rust*

JUSTICE IS BLIND...AND NOW, DEAF AND DUMB

Paul Conrad. Copyright, 1991, Los Angeles Times.
Reprinted with permission.

First Amendment Foundation

1313 West 8th Street, Suite 313, Los Angeles, California 90017   213/484-6661

Dear Friend of the First Amendment Foundation:

Enclosed you will find your order for Professor Richard Curry's hardhitting and timely book:

Uncertain Future:

T H O U G H T   C O N T R O L

and

R E P R E S S I O N

R E A G A N - B U S H   E R A

We will welcome your suggestions as to how we can give the book the widest possible distribution, especially to students, libraries, and groups unaware of the dangers to their rights.

** If you will send us a list of addresses of friends to whom you would like the book to be sent, our office volunteers will do the mailing.

Enclose $15 each ($12 + $3 postage for each person - or for 10 or more see discount rate on the last page of the book).

Seattle, Washington

Walter M. Kearns
Woodland Hills, California
TREASURER

Elizabeth Poe Kerby
Los Angeles, California

Chuck Lapine
Washington, District of Columbia

Maryann Mabaffey
Detroit, Michigan

Nancy G. McDermid
San Francisco, California

Victor Navasky
New York, New York

Gifford Phillips
New York, New York

Ramona Ripston
Los Angeles, California

Frank L. Rosen
Chicago, Illinois

Rabbi David Saperstein
Washington, District of Columbia

Reverend C.T. Vivian
Atlanta, Georgia

oward J. Unterberger, Esq.
LEGAL COUNSEL

Frank Wilkinson
EXECUTIVE DIRECTOR

Madonna Harrison
CONSULTANT ON MANAGEMENT

had a devastating impact on low income women since seventy percent of all abortions had previously taken place in these clinics; but equally important, it clearly establishes the principle that "he who pays the piper calls the tune." If such views are applied to other aspects of American life which involve federal funding—e.g., the arts, education, housing, transportation—the damage to First Amendment values and freedom of choice will be incalculable.

Mr. Rehnquist's opinion that the principle would never be applied to universities is not reassuring. Moreover, the Bush administration's subsequent revision of clinic guidelines to exempt doctors was disingenuous at best since only a small percentage of the information or counselling on abortion was provided by physicians.

At first glance, *Barnes* v. *Glen Theater* (1991), appears to have little in common with *Webster* and *Rust*. *Barnes*, after all, upheld the constitutionality of an Indiana law prohibiting nude dancing. What has nude dancing to do with abortion? Nothing. But, one of the underlying principles involved in all three cases is the same.

In *Barnes*, the Court ruled that Indiana legislators could require female dancers to wear "at least pasties and G-strings" because "protecting order and morality" was a "compelling state interest." The *common principle* in all three cases, therefore, is *the right of government*, whether state or national, *to restrict freedom of speech*. Whether such restrictions are based upon the need to protect "order and morality" or stem from making "policy choices" or "value judgments" in allocating public funds, the end result is the same. Both *Barnes* and *Rust* were decided on the basis of 5-4 decisions, and in each case, the deciding vote was cast by Justice Souter, who replaced Justice Brennan on the Supreme Court in early 1989. How ironic that Justice Brennan's "last hurrah" was his majority opinion in *Texas* v. *Johnson* (1988), which stated that flag burning was symbolic speech and, as such, was protected by the First Amendment. In light of the Supreme Court's more recent rulings in *Webster*, *Rust*, and *Barnes*, one is compelled to wonder not only how far the New Majority is willing to go in restricting First Amendment principles, but how long it will take for the "New Leviathan" to become "lord and master of all it surveys."

The *Webster* decision, in addition to placing restrictions upon abortion counselling, had two other major results. In 1973, the Supreme Court, in *Roe* v. *Wade* declared that a woman's right to abortion was a *fundamental right*, which in legal terms meant that it was comparable to the right to vote. *Webster*, and indeed, *Rust*, indicate that a majority of the current Supreme Court Justices now view the right to have an abortion as less than *fundamental*. The *Webster* case, therefore, encouraged "pro-life" activists to lobby for more restrictive laws. They were successful in Idaho, Louisiana, Utah, Pennsylvania, and the territory of Guam. Constitutional challenges to all of these laws were mounted. But the Pennsylvania case, *Planned Parenthood of Southeastern Pennsylvania* v. *Robert P. Casey*, was placed on the Court's docket for adjudication during its 1991-92 term. Among other things, the Pennsylvania law required a 24-hour waiting period, and required young women under 18 either to notify one parent or secure a parental notification waiver from a judge.

Many "pro-choice" and "pro-life" advocates, in light of the Court's rulings in *Webster* and *Rust*, believed that the High Court would use *Planned Parenthood* to overturn *Roe*. Moreover, the reasoning of the Third Federal Circuit Court of Appeals, which upheld most of the Pennsylvania law's provisions, had amazed supporters and opponents alike. *Roe* v. *Wade*, the circuit court declared, was no longer a useful precedent. In addition to evaluating *Webster*, the circuit court judges had studied the views of all current members of the Supreme Court on abortion. Since a majority had "written in one way or another that *Roe* was wrongly decided," the Third Circuit Court's decision, therefore, had been made without reference to it.[44]

By a 5-4 majority, the Supreme Court in *Planned Parenthood*, upheld the constitutionality of all of the Pennsylvania law's restrictions with the exception that wives were not required to inform their husbands of their decision to have an abortion. The Court's majority also replaced *Roe*'s "trimester system" with an "undue burden" standard that reaffirmed the right of women to choose an abortion subject to rules, regulations, and procedures imposed by state legislatures that did not impose an "undue burden" or a "substantial obstacle" that would eliminate choice.

The Court, however, failed to define what it meant by an "undue burden" or a "substantial obstacle." What the decision really means, therefore, as attorney Katherine Kolbert phrased it, "is full employment for lawyers."[45] It will take years of litigation to determine precisely what the law means. "Pro-life" advocates will attempt to impose rules and regulations that will make it even more difficult for women to get an abortion. "Pro-choice" lawyers, on the other hand, will get involved in litigation which tries to demonstrate for example, that 24-hour or 72-hour waiting periods, do, in fact impose an "undue burden" for poor women living in rural areas. In Pennsylvania, for example, only eight of the state's sixty-seven counties have hospitals or clinics willing to perform abortions. The added time and expense imposed by a waiting period will make it extremely difficult for some women who want an abortion to get it.[46]

Susan Estrich, a law professor and Governor Dukakis's campaign manager in 1988, looked at the issues from a somewhat different angle. "If *Roe* v. *Wade* is dead," Estrich began,

> and it is in much of America, it is not because of what the Supreme Court did Monday, but because of the success of terrorist tactics [utilized by Operation Rescue, for one example] that have left 83 percent of America's counties without a single clinic or hospital willing to perform an abortion. That is a 'substantial obstacle,' and while neither the Court nor the Pennsylvania legislature may be directly responsible, the rules imposed by states must be scrutinized in the light of the burden they impose.[47]

The most surprising aspect of the Court's decision not to overturn *Roe*'s principal finding—that is, the right of a woman to choose—was the reasoning of Justices Souter, Kennedy, and O'Connor. Although Souter was the primary author of the majority opinion it was also signed by Kennedy and O'Connor. Justices Blackmun and Stevens concurred in part, thus providing the 5-4 majority.

The decision was 60 pages long, the first 16 of which provided a sustained commentary on the importance of *stare decisis* and the legitimacy of the Supreme Court as an institution. For example, one key passage stated:

> A decision to overrule *Roe*'s essential holding under existing circumstances would address error, if error there was, at the cost of both profound and unnecessary damage to the court's legitimacy, and the Nation's commitment to the rule of law. It is therefore imperative to adhere to the essence of *Roe*'s original decision, and we do so today.

Another passage declared that if precedents were reversed without a compelling reason to do so, the "legitimacy of the court would fade with the frequency of its vacillation."

EQUAL · JUSTICE · UNDER · LAW

HABEAS CORPSE

Paul Conrad. Copyright, 1991, Los Angeles Times.
Reprinted with permission.

THOUGHT CONTROL AND REPRESSION

Some commentators have argued that the votes of Justices Souter, O'Connor, and Kennedy on *Planned Parenthood, Lee* v. *Weisman* (which banned school prayer at high school graduation ceremonies), and *Wright* v. *West*, a *habeas corpus* case, in the closing days of the 1991-92 session, demonstrates the emergence of these Reagan-Bush appointees as a moderating force that has limited the Court's move to the right. Suffice it to say here that most of the evidence cited in this chapter demonstrates that Justices O'Connor, Souter, and Kennedy have all played a critically important role since 1989 in the New Right's judicial counterrevolution that has transformed American constitutional law in only three years' time. It remains to be seen whether or not Justices Souter, O'Connor and Kennedy are going to form a moderate voting bloc that will serve to limit an even more radical shift to the right than the one they played such a major role in producing.[48]

Reducing Habeas Corpus Petitions by State Inmates

Until recently, convicted felons incarcerated in state prisons could challenge the legality or constitutionality of their convictions by filing *habeas corpus* petitions and thereby securing a review in the federal courts. Two cases, decided in 1963, established modern precedents on *habeas corpus* issues on both procedural and substantive grounds. Both decisions, moreover, contained safeguards against abuse of the writ. What emerged in *Sanders* v. *United States* was essentially a ''good-faith'' standard which permitted successive petitions to be judged on their merits. The other case, *Fay* v. *Noia*, established the ''deliberate by-pass'' test, which stated that a petitioner, whose claims had not been heard on the state level for good and sufficient reason, could reasonably expect a hearing at the federal level. But Justice Brennan, who wrote the majority opinion in *Fay*, made it clear that abuse would not be tolerated. ''Nothing in the traditions of *habeas corpus*,'' Brennan wrote, ''requires the federal courts to tolerate needless piecemeal litigation, or to entertain collateral proceedings whose only purpose is to vex, harass, or delay.''

Sanders, which embraced the Court's ''deliberate by-pass'' test in *Fay*, provided the basis for congressional action in 1966. As Justice Marshall explained: ''Congress has affirmatively ratified the *Sanders* good-faith standard in the governing statute and procedural rules, thereby insulating that standard from judicial repeal.''

Chief Justice Rehnquist, who has long been opposed to the standards contained in *Sanders* and *Fay* attempted, unsuccessfully, to persuade Congress in 1990 to change the law and the procedural rules governing *habeas corpus*. As a result, the Rehnquist court, which in the past has vociferously denounced "judicial activism," proceeded to use its power in 1991 and again in 1992, not merely to overturn established *habeas corpus* precedents, but to declare statutory law on the subject unconstitutional.

In *McClesky* v. *Zant* (1991), the New Majority adopted a "cause and prejudice" standard which makes more than one federal *habeas corpus* hearing virtually impossible. In filing second or subsequent claims, a prisoner must show "cause" as to why new claims were not included in earlier petitions. The catch here is the definition of "cause." If, as Justice Marshall observed in his dissenting opinion, a prisoner's attorney, in drafting an earlier petition, failed to include a claim because it was based on a "reasonable perception that a particular claim is without factual or legal foundation, that does not excuse the failure to raise that claim. . . ." *Cause* exists *only* when counsel can demonstrate "that he was impeded by some objective factor external to the defense, such as governmental interference or the reasonable unavailability of the factual basis for the claim. . . ." Equally important, the prisoner must also demonstrate that "actual prejudice" resulted "from the errors of which he complains." What is *actual prejudice*? If a prisoner cannot demonstrate that the errors involved affected the outcome of his case, a federal judge is not required to hold an evidential hearing unless it can be demonstrated "that a fundamental miscarriage of justice—the conviction of an innocent person—would result from a failure to entertain the claim."

In an even more crushing decision, *Coleman* v. *Thompson* (1991), the Court ruled that Robert K. Coleman, a death row inmate in Virginia, was not entitled to even one hearing in the federal courts. Coleman's lawyers were three days late in filing a *habeas corpus* petition to Virginia's Supreme Court. His attorney's negligence did not constitute *cause* for granting Coleman a review at the federal level. The petitioner, O'Connor said, "must bear the risk of attorney error." Why so? Because O'Connor said, *Fay* v. *Noia* "was based on a conception of federal-state relations that undervalued the importance of state procedural rules." "We now recognize," O'Connor continued, "the important interest in finality served by state procedural rules, and the significant harm to the states that results from the failure of federal courts to respect them." "This case is at an end," she concluded.

In a vigorous dissenting opinion, Justice Harry A. Blackmun, denounced the New Majority's "crusade" to deny state prisoners access to the federal courts. *Coleman*, he continued, "marks the nadir of the Court's recent *habeas* jurisprudence." The Court, Blackmun concluded, "is creating a byzantine morass of arbitrary, unnecessary, and unjustifiable impediments to the vindication of Federal rights."

In still another *habeas corpus* case, *Keeney* v. *Tamayo-Reyes* (1992), the Court ruled that a Cuban-born inmate was not entitled to a federal *habeas corpus* review despite the fact the Spanish translation of a plea agreement was inadequate. The United States Court of Appeals for the Ninth Circuit, invoking the "deliberate by-pass standard," had concluded that since the petitioner's lawyer, in his state court appeal, failed to explain the essential facts about the circumstances of the plea, especially the inadequacy of the Spanish translation, the petitioner was entitled to a review. Justice Byron R. White who wrote the Supreme Court's majority opinion, argued, in an obvious reference to the *Coleman* decision and to *McClesky*, that attorney error does not qualify as a valid *cause*. White emphasized the desirability of *finality*, which the "cause and prejudice" standard provided. The "deliberate by-pass" standard, he declared, "dramatically increases the opportunity to relitigate a conviction" by state courts whenever lawyer error was involved.

The case was remarkable, not for its conclusions, but for the fact that Justices O'Connor and Kennedy dissented. Kennedy, who wrote the majority opinion in *McClesky*, declared in his *Keeney* dissent that the petition was proper in procedural terms, and that the case fell into a category that "Federal courts are bound to decide in order to protect constitutional rights." "We ought not to take steps," he added, "which diminish the likelihood that those courts will base their legal decision on an accurate assessment of the facts."

O'Connor, on the other hand, who wrote the majority opinion in *Coleman*, penned an amazing dissent. "While we may deprive portions of our own prior decisions of any effect," she said, "we may not, of course, do the same with portions of statutes." This decision, she argued, invalidated part of the federal *habeas corpus* law of 1966. As we observed earlier, this is precisely what the Court did in *McClesky*; and O'Connor cast her vote with the majority.

Linda Greenhouse, an astute and articulate analyst of Supreme Court cases, states

> That both Justice O'Connor and Justice Kennedy, two of the Court's leaders in the campaign to restrict *habeas corpus*, cast dissenting votes [in *Keeney*] was a powerful indication of how far the Court has gone. The two newest Justices, David H. Souter and Clarence Thomas, voted silently with the majority, an even more powerful indication of how much farther the Court is likely to go.

The Rights of Criminals and Criminal Defendants

In a 1985 case, *Oregon* v. *Elstad*, the Supreme Court ruled that whereas a confession obtained by police without reading the suspect his *Miranda* rights was invalid, a second confession, obtained after Elstad had been informed of his rights, was valid. As University of Michigan law professor Yale Kamisar informed Nat Hentoff: "It's a silly concept—telling someone that he can remain silent and has a right to a lawyer after he's already made an incriminating statement." The fact remains, however, that the doctrine of "excluding the fruit of the poisonous tree" no longer applies to *Miranda* violations. Little wonder that Justice Brennan, in his dissenting opinion, wrote that the Supreme Court was becoming "increasingly irrelevant in the protection of individual rights."

Beginning in 1989, in a series of 5-4 decisions, the Rehnquist Court, began to confirm the worst fears of civil libertarians. In *Penry* v. *Lynaugh*, the Court permitted the execution of a mentally retarded person and in *Stanford* v. *Kentucky*, it allowed the execution of a sixteen year old boy. In both cases, the Court rejected defense counsel's arguments that the death penalty in these cases constituted cruel and unusual punishment.

In another Eighth Amendment case, *Harmelin* v. *Michigan* (1991), the Court upheld the constitutionality of a Michigan law under which Ronald A. Harmelin, a first time offender, convicted of possessing 1.5 pounds of cocaine, was sentenced to life in prison without the possibility of parole. Although the Supreme Court has never defined cruel and unusual punishment with exactitude, previous cases have reflected two general principles: the idea of proportionality and that of comparison. Proportionality means that the punishment should fit the crime, whereas comparison refers to the terms of the law in other states for similar offenses. In Alabama, for example, the same offense called for a five year prison term, and even under federal law, Harmelin would have been sentenced to ten years imprisonment.

The majority opinion, written by Justice Scalia and joined by Chief Justice Rehnquist, arrogantly dismissed Harmelin's Eighth Amendment claim by concluding that the principle of proportionality applied only to death sentences. Previous decisions that concluded otherwise ought to be reconsidered. Although Justices O'Connor, Kennedy, and Souter failed to adopt Scalia's and Rehnquist's position on proportionality, they argued that the punishment did fit the crime. Justice Kennedy's opinion, which was joined by Justices O'Connor and Souter, said that it was "false to the point of absurdity" to argue that possessing enough cocaine to yield 32,500 to 65,000 doses was a "non-violent crime."

"Do such jurists really deserve the label conservative?" the *Hartford Courant* editorialized. "They are surely radical activists and they certainly have political agendas." It is not "the job of Supreme Court Justices," the editorial concluded, "to cheer on a drug war or to assure the state that it will always have enough power to intimidate citizens. . . ." In short, it is the job of law enforcement officers and prosecutors to deal with the drug problem and the job of the High Court "to stand apart from political agendas and to concern itself with interpreting the Constitution." Justice Marshall once commented that a constitutional exception for drug cases does not exist. Members of the Court's New Majority clearly think otherwise.

Three other 1991 cases, two of which were also decided by 5-4 majorities, also deserve analysis. In *Wilson* v. *Seiter*, the Supreme Court concluded that deplorable prison conditions such as overcrowding, poor sanitation, and exposure to violence did not constitute cruel and unusual punishment unless prison administrators acted with "deliberate indifference" to the plight of prisoners. The Court's decision, however, did not state precisely how a prison official's state of mind can be gauged with any degree of accuracy.

In *Arizona* v. *Fulminante*, the other 5-4 decision, the Supreme Court ruled that "coerced confessions," did not invalidate convictions if it could be proved that sufficient evidence existed, apart from the confession itself, to convict a defendant. In that event a coerced confession must be considered as nothing more than a "harmless error." This decision overturned part of *Chapman* v. *California* (1967) which ruled that three errors—coerced confessions, absence of counsel, and a biased judge—automatically invalidated a conviction. In this particular case, Fulminante was awarded a new trial. But the Court's new standard appears to send a not so subtle message to law enforcement officials that police brutality will, in some cases, be condoned.

Another landmark case, *Payne* v. *Tennessee* (1991), reversed established precedents regarding the use of "victim impact" statements —that is, a discussion of the impact of a murder on the victim's family in attempting to influence a jury's decision as to whether or not the death sentence should be imposed. In *Booth* v. *Maryland* (1987), and again in *Gathers* v. *South Carolina* (1989), the Court ruled that the use of such testimony was not permissible. In *Payne*, Chief Justice Rehnquist, who wrote the majority decision, stated that barring such evidence "unfairly weighted the scales in a capital trial" in favor of defendants. In an angry dissent, delivered only two hours before announcing his retirement, Justice Marshall declared: "Neither the law nor the facts supporting *Booth* and *Gathers* underwent any change in the last four years. Only the personnel of the Court did." Marshall went on to say that although *stare decisis* is not an "inexorable command," this "Court has repeatedly stressed that fidelity to precedent is fundamental to 'a society governed by the rule of law.'" The Court, he concluded, ought not to abandon precedent without "special justification."

Justice John Paul Stevens, who also dissented, wrote that he shared Marshall's concern about the Court's "trivialization of the doctrine of *stare decisis*." But even if *Booth* and *Gathers* had never existed, Stevens declared that *Payne* was "a sharp break with past decisions." "Until today," he wrote, decisions to impose capital punishment were "based solely on evidence that tends to inform the jury about the character of the offense and the character of the defendant." Victim impact evidence, Justice Stevens concluded, serves no other purpose than "to encourage jurors to decide in favor of death rather than life on the basis of their emotions rather than reason."

Civil Liberties and the "War" on Drugs

In 1982 President Reagan declared "war" on the sale and use of illegal drugs in the United States. The seriousness of the problem is not subject to question. But neither the Reagan nor Bush administrations have emphasized the root causes of drug abuse—poverty, racism, massive unemployment, urban decay, homelessness, and alienation, among other factors, which contribute not only to drug abuse but crimes against persons and property. Under both Reagan and Bush, drastic cuts in social services—including funds for the treatment and rehabilitation of drug addicts—serve only to compound the problems involved.

Instead of providing solutions, the Reagan administration's drug policy included a massive increase in the prosecutorial power, personnel, and funding of those federal agencies charged with destroying the drug menace. A compliant Congress cooperated by passing laws such as the Comprehensive Crime Control Act of 1984, and the Anti-Drug Abuse laws of 1986 and 1988 which emphasized "eradication" rather than a combination of social, economic, and law enforcement programs providing long-range solutions.

The centerpiece of President Bush's program was the 1988 Anti-Drug Abuse Act, passed in November 1988. This legislation created the Office of National Drug Control Policy with a presidential appointee (commonly known as a "drug czar") empowered to coordinate all federal enforcement mechanisms. The law also provides for more specific procedures for the seizure of assets under civil as well as criminal proceedings. The evidentiary requirements in civil cases are not nearly as stringent as those in criminal indictments. In criminal cases, a person, presumably, is not guilty until convicted by a jury. In civil cases, however, a suspected drug dealer must prove his innocence to avoid forfeiture.

In Connecticut, for example, an overzealous federal prosecutor confiscated the home of aged grandparents who were unaware that their grandson, who lived with them, was an alleged drug dealer. In this particular case, it eventually came to light that the federal prosecutor's own son was accused of using her car and home to sell drugs. Although this prosecutor was transferred to another department, her property was not confiscated. If it had been, she, like most victims, would have been eligible to get it back only by buying it at public auction.

Our primary purpose here, however, is not to analyze the complexities, anomalies, and contradictions in federal drug enforcement legislation and policies. It is, rather, to document the complicity of the Supreme Court in legitimizing the draconian drug policies utilized by state and federal law enforcement officials. As we shall soon see, the constitutionality of some of these policies and procedures has been challenged—albeit unsuccessfully—in the courts.

Most of the Supreme Court's Fourth Amendment drug cases were rendered, predictably enough, between 1989-91. Two critically important cases, however, were decided earlier: *U.S.* v. *Ross* (1982) and *California* v. *Ciraola* (1986).

In *Ross*, police officers, acting on a tip from an informant, stopped and searched an automobile. In process, they opened a paper bag and a zippered pouch containing incriminating evidence without obtaining a warrant. The respondent's pre-trial motion to suppress this evidence was denied and so, Ross was convicted. The United States Court of Appeals for the Third Circuit, however, reversed Ross's conviction—arguing that whereas the police had probable cause for stopping the automobile, they exceeded their lawful authority by failing to obtain a warrant to open the containers.

The Supreme Court disagreed. Justice Stevens, who wrote the majority opinion, stated that when police officers have probable cause to search a vehicle, they can conduct a warrantless search of its contents, including all containers and packages, that may conceal the object of the search. But Stevens went even farther by declaring a police officer's estimation of probable cause was equivalent to a warrant.

Justice Marshall, as usual, was quite pointed in his dissenting opinion. "In adopting today's new rule," Marshall wrote, "the majority opinion shows contempt for these Fourth Amendment values, ignores this Court's precedents, is internally inconsistent, and produces anomalous and unjust consequences."

Four years later, in *California* v. *Ciraola*, the Court's majority validated the issuance of a warrant to search Ciraola's property on the basis of evidence obtained by warrantless aerial surveillance of his backyard. Thus, the "reasonable expectation of privacy," mandated by the Fourth Amendment became, in this case, a casualty of technological innovation.

Eliminating warrant requirements, and allowing law enforcement officers to determine the meaning of "probable cause" without having to submit evidence to judges for an independent review, obviously constitutes a major change in Fourth Amendment jurisprudence. Even more radical in terms of its implications is the Court's decision in *Florida* v. *Rodriguez* (1989). The probable cause standard, which was weakened in *Ross*, was replaced by a new category which the Court called "articulable suspicion." Under the terms of *Rodriguez*, individuals could be detained and questioned if "articulable suspicion" exists to suggest that "a person has committed or is about to commit a crime."

What is "articulable suspicion?" By any measure, it's a vague standard. In *Rodriguez*, the defendant's rapid walking pace and his air of insecurity provided the rationale for detention. In future, it might be a result of wearing sandals on a cold day, wearing tennis shoes with a three piece suit, stuttering when paying cash for an airline ticket to Peoria, or having a skull and cross-bones tattoo engraved on one's left ear lobe. In short, "articulable suspicion," is little more than a subjective reaction by law enforcement officers whose reactions vary according to time, place, circumstance, and body temperature.

Our consideration of the Supreme Court's role in fighting the "war on drugs" ends with an analysis of *Skinner* v. *Railway Labor Executives Association* (1989). This case, which falls into the "special needs" category, requires railway employees to submit to both urinalysis and blood tests immediately after major accidents. Justice Kennedy, writing for the majority, rejected the idea that probable cause or some type of individualized suspicion standard was needed to justify these types of invasive procedures. The railway employees' privacy interests, Kennedy argued, were outweighed by the competing governmental interest in railway safety.

Such drastic action, however, serves to obscure the fact that railway accidents often result from causes other than drug abuse—e.g. faulty equipment and inadequate inspection. It also ignores the fact that the indiscriminate use of blood samples can result in studies that reveal some of the most intimate aspects of a person's life—not only eating and drinking habits, for example, but one's disposition towards certain types of disease including epilepsy, diabetes, and clinical depression. Obviously, obtaining such information is not the purpose of *Skinner*; but requiring citizens to provide blood samples to government officials without probable cause establishes a precedent which, in time, and under somewhat different circumstances, can conceivably be applied to other issues.

Justice Marshall, in another of his penetrating dissents, argues

U.S. SUPREME COURT UPHOLDS REVERSE DISCRIMINATION CASE.

Paul Conrad. Copyright, 1989, Los Angeles Times.
Reprinted with permission.

that "special needs" justifications in *Skinner* unnecessarily compromises the "probable cause" standard. For example, no spoilation of blood and urine samples occur "if [they are] properly collected and preserved." There is no justification, therefore, to "dispense with the warrant requirement." The majority's "special needs" justification in this or any other case is simply "unprincipled and dangerous." Who could doubt, Marshall wryly observed, that if law enforcement officers were "freed from the constraints of Fourth Amendment for just one day . . . the resulting convictions and incarcerations would probably prevent thousands of fatalities?" In a free society, however, constitutional safeguards exist to protect the rights of individuals against unwarranted intrusions regardless of whether short-sighted or authoritarian policies "will save money, save lives, or make the trains run on time." "The precious liberties of our citizens," Marshall concluded, are "the first, and worst casualty of the war on drugs."[49]

Employment Discrimination Cases

The Civil Rights Act of 1964 made employment discrimination illegal. Its terminology on this point was sufficiently vague, however, that it permitted many employers to use "neutral" screening devices (a euphemism for discriminatory practices) in hiring their work force. For example, height and weight qualifications denied most women an opportunity to become law enforcement officers, and the requirement of a high school diploma denied many members of minority groups an opportunity to compete for assembly line jobs. The American workplace, therefore, was segregated by sex, race, or both. All that changed in 1971 when the Supreme Court delivered its landmark decision, *Griggs* v. *Duke Power, Inc.* As one commentator phrased it, *Griggs* "deserves more credit for integrating America's workplace than any other law case." What the Court did, in short, was to establish a "disparate impact" standard. If statistical analysis revealed that a disproportionate number of minorities or women were excluded from certain jobs, a company was required to demonstrate, in court, that the qualifications were not only work-related but a "business necessity." Other important cases, including *Albermarle Paper Co.* v. *Moody* (1975) and *Dothard* v. *Rawlinson* (1977), not only strengthened the *Griggs* precedent but accelerated the process of integration.

The Supreme Court's New Majority, when it came to power in 1989, lost little time in reversing *Griggs*. In *Wards Cove Packing Co.* v. *Atonio*, the Court, by a 5-4 majority, shifted the burden of proof from employers to employees. The *Ward's Cove* decision, in fact, was a mirror image of *Griggs*. Employees were now required to prove that job qualifications were not work-related and were not a result of "business necessity." Statistics could be introduced as evidence in court only if employees "could also identify specific acts that caused the statistical disparity."

In 1989, the High Court also decided several other discrimination cases. In *Martin* v. *Wilks*, the Court, in another 5-4 decision, ruled that white firefighters in Birmingham, Alabama could challenge a court-approved affirmative action settlement in which the fire department was required to hire and promote more blacks.

In a related case, *Jett* v. *Dallas Independent School District*, the Court ruled, once again by a 5-4 margin, that the Civil Rights Act of 1866 could no longer be used to bring damage suits against cities which, allegedly, were guilty of racial discrimination. The act itself, however, was not invalidated, but in *Patterson* v. *McLean Credit Union*, the Court ruled that the act applied only to hiring practices and not to on-the-job discrimination.

. Attention must also be called to two other cases decided in 1989. In *Croson* v. *City of Richmond*, the Court invalidated a city of Richmond ordinance that channeled thirty percent of public work funds to minority-owned construction companies. The ordinance, the Court ruled, violated the rights of white contractors who were being denied equal protection under the law.

In light of the Supreme Court's decisions to reverse or narrow the application of established precedents in discrimination cases, it is difficult to explain the Court's ruling in *Hopkins* v. *Price Waterhouse*. In this case, which involved three different majority opinions, the Court declared that in cases involving individuals, rather than groups, employers were required to demonstrate that discrimination, based on race, sex, or age, was not involved in their decision not to hire or promote someone. Linda Greenhouse observes that the *Hopkins* decision obviously reflects a "sharply different approach" from that taken in *Wards Cove*. But cases involving efforts by "individual plaintiffs trying to prove that they were singled out for discriminatory treatment" is a "category," Greenhouse concludes, "to which conservatives on and off the Court have remained fairly sympathetic."[50]

The Civil Rights Act of 1991

The *Wards Cove* decision, however, not only produced a public outcry from organizations dedicated to protecting the rights of minorities and women, but resulted in the creation of a bipartisan congressional coalition which passed the Civil Rights Act of 1990. Its primary objective was to restore the "disparate impact" standard repudiated by the New Majority in *Ward's Cove*. Unfortunately, the margin of victory was not sufficiently large to override President Bush's veto. The president repeatedly, but wrongly, denounced the act as a "quota bill."

In 1991, Congress tried again, and after a long and rancorous debate, passed the Civil Rights Act of 1991. This time, the president signed the act into law. Mr. Bush, administration officials, and conservative Republicans expressed satisfaction with the elimination of a "quota system" which the bill had never contained. Only the unwary, the unprincipled, or the uninformed ever took that position in the first place. What the law did, among other things, was to restore the *Griggs* standard. Hiring criteria, the law stated, must have a "manifest relationship to the requirements for effective job performance."

Mr. Bush, however, had a variety of political reasons for signing the 1991 act which had not existed the year before. For one thing, it allowed the president and other conservative Republicans to differentiate their position on race from that of David Duke. For another, the law allowed women, for the first time, to collect compensatory and punitive damages in sex bias cases. By claiming some of the credit for this provision, Mr. Bush hoped to minimize the political damage done, especially among women voters, by Professor Anita Hill's allegations of sexual harassment during Justice Thomas's confirmation hearings. Even so, the law, which contained no limits for monetary awards in cases involving racial discrimination, limited awards in sex bias cases to $300,000.

With congressional Democrats and the Bush administration both claiming victory, the president, two days before signing the Civil Rights Act of 1991, found himself engulfed in still another firestorm. White House counsel C. Boyden Gray, a close presidential adviser,

Paul Conrad. Copyright, 1991, Los Angeles Times.
Reprinted with permission.

circulated a draft of a proposed executive order, which stated that all executive-branch agencies should "terminate" programs giving preference in hiring to minorities and women. The proposed order also stated that federal advisory guidelines regarding compliance with anti-discrimination laws by businesses would be abolished.[51]

Senator John Danforth, the chief Republican sponsor of the Civil Rights Act, informed White House Chief of Staff, John Sununu, that the proposed executive order "was a disaster." It would "rub a national wound raw." After protests by Danforth, other Republican members of Congress, and some agency heads, President Bush ordered the most controversial language deleted. Even so, Marlin Fitzwater, the president's press secretary, refused to disavow the substance of Gray's memorandum. After further review, Fitzwater said, the Bush administration might yet decide to curtail federal affirmative action programs and guidelines.[52]

New York Governor Mario Cuomo remarked: "What this proves to you is that they're not playing from any set of rules or principles." But the next day, at the Rose Garden ceremony, President Bush, in signing the act into law, appeared to be unflappable. "For the past few years," he said, "the issue of civil rights legislation has divided Americans. No more." The president went on to say: "Today we celebrate a law that will fight the evil of discrimination, while also building bridges of harmony between Americans of all races, sexes, creeds and backgrounds."

The sound and fury has subsided, at least momentarily, and most commentators agree that the new law overturned a number of Supreme Court decisions including *Ward's Cove* v. *Atonio* and *Equal Employment Opportunity Commission* v. *American Arabian Oil Co.*, a case in which the Supreme Court ruled that anti-discrimination laws did not apply to American citizens who worked for American companies overseas. Other commentators, especially lawyers specializing in job discrimination cases, observed that the Civil Rights Act of 1991 contains so many confusing and ambiguous provisions that it will take years of litigation to determine precisely what some aspects of the law actually mean.[53]

Steven A. Holmes, a reporter who writes on legal issues, discusses several important unresolved issues raised by the act.[54] First, "Is the law retroactive?" Does it apply to cases that were pending when the law was passed, or only to "new cases?" Second, the law permits "women, the disabled and members of religious minorities" to receive up to $300,000 in punitive and compensatory damages. But the law is not clear as to "whether it means $300,000 per lawsuit or $300,000 for each allegation." In addition, can "employers legally continue programs that favor women and minority members in hiring and promotion?" The law's language is both confusing and contradictory. Moreover, what is the law's impact on "affirmative action for state and local governments and school boards that base hiring and promotion on civil service tests?" Beyond this, Holmes points out that the effects of the law on voluntary affirmative action programs—that is, those that were not court ordered, are "particularly troubling." Although the law says that it protects programs that are "in accordance with the law," it fails "to define that phrase." Does it refer to past Supreme Court decisions that have upheld "the use of race or sex in hiring or promotions?" Or does it refer to the new law which "says the consideration of race or sex is now illegal?"

Thus, the Civil Rights Act of 1991, which has reversed the Supreme Court's New Majority on some issues, has apparently created the proverbial "can of worms" that, in the future, will provide the current members of the High Court with sufficient latitude to interpret the law in new and perhaps unanticipated ways.

The law's ambiguities and contradictions even suggest that if the timing and political astuteness of White House counsel C. Boyden Gray are subject to question, the substance of the proposed executive order he drafted on terminating federal affirmative action programs for women and minority groups may not actually conflict with the Civil Rights Act of 1991. If Congress fails to clarify some of the law's provisions—as predictably it will in the short run—then the law becomes the province of the Federal courts, where it faces an uncertain future.

The Imperial Presidency

The Iran-Contra Scandal

Thus far, our analysis has centered primarily on the domestic aspects of the Reagan administration's massive assaults on civil liberties in the name of "national security." Yet, the Reagan administration's conduct of foreign policy also has important domestic ramifications. Domestic and foreign policy initiatives are, in fact, inextricably intertwined. Nowhere was the Reagan administration's distrust of openness and democratic processes better reflected than in its Central American policies.

Among other things, the Iran-Contra hearings revealed not only a basic distrust of the American people and of Congress but also an insensitivity to the principle of separation of powers itself. This principle includes, of course, the accountability of executive branch agencies to congressional oversight committees. The president, as commander in chief, is charged with conducting foreign policy. But the Congress, as mandated by the Constitution, does have a critical role to play in the foreign policy sphere. When scholars refer to the growth of the "imperial presidency" since the Second World War, they refer, obviously, to the enormous growth of presidential power in the conduct of foreign affairs. As regards Central America, however, and especially Nicaragua, Congress reasserted its constitutional powers with vigor. The Boland Amendment provides a case in point.

The Boland Amendment, which is often referred to in the press as a "congressional ban," was in fact a law—a rider attached to the Defense Appropriations Act of 1985 signed by President Reagan. The amendment stated: "During the fiscal year 1985, no funds available to the Central Intelligence Agency, or any other agency or entity of the United States involved in intelligence activities may be obligated or expended for the purpose of supporting, directly or indirectly, military or paramilitary operations" against the Sandinista government.[55]

Although President Reagan admitted that he signed an order authorizing the sale of weapons to Iran, he has consistently denied culpability in the diversion of funds to the Contras. No evidence gathered by the Tower Commission or the congressional Iran-Contra Committee proved otherwise. But President Reagan, in response to charges that the National Security Council had violated the Boland Amendment by secretly supplying the Contras, stated to a group of magazine editors:

> My interpretation was that it [the Boland Amendment] was not restrictive on the National Security Adviser or National Security Council. . . . I believe that the NSC is not an intelligence operation; it's simply advisory to me. And there is nothing in the Boland Amendment that would keep me from asking other people to help [e.g., private individuals, the Sultan of Brunei, Saudia Arabia, and South Africa].[56]

Such a defense, according to congressional critics and many legal experts, is not valid. Even Robert McFarlane, the former national security adviser, admitted to the Iran- Contra Committee that the NSC was indeed an agency involved in intelligence activities and thus subject to the restrictions imposed by the Boland Amendment. Even more telling are the terms of President Reagan's Executive Order 12333. It designated the NSC "as the highest executive branch entity that provides review of, guidance for, and direction to the conduct of all national and foreign intelligence [and] counterintelligence" operations.[57]

Numerous commentators have observed that President Reagan's lack of knowledge that illegal funds were diverted to the Contras by some of his top aides is a shocking revelation—nearly as shocking as involvement itself. The fact that the president's interpretations of E.O. 12333 reveal ignorance of the contents of his own edict must be placed in the same category. Executive orders, it must be remembered, have the force of law.

It cannot be too strongly emphasized, moreover, that the Constitution states that the "executive branch shall faithfully execute the laws of the United States." When a president (or members of his administration) unilaterally decides which laws to execute and which to ignore, he places himself above the law which, in turn, degrades and threatens the democratic process itself. As Peter Rodino, former chair of the House Judiciary Committee and a member of the Iran-Contra Select Committee, phrased it:

> The fundamental question posed, just as in the Watergate crisis, has to do with the Executive's misunderstanding of the rule of law. Nothing undermines our representative system of government more than actions taken by officials entrusted with the reins of government, which even for purposes believed to be good, are designed to set aside the law, distort, or ignore it. . . . Only our adherence to the rule of law can, in the end, restore the people's trust which has been so sorely impaired.[58]

Reagan's Fascination with Martial Law

Perhaps the most startling disclosure to emerge from the Iran-Contra scandal was the Reagan administration's contingency plans for imposing martial law. Alfonso Chardy, a reporter for the *Miami Herald*, revealed in July 1987 that Lt. Col. Oliver North, while serving on the National Security Council's staff, had worked with FEMA (Federal Emergency Management Agency) on a plan to suspend the Bill of Rights by imposing martial law in the event of "national opposition to a U.S. military invasion abroad." John Russell, a Justice Department spokesperson, denied the charges. Russell stated: "We have the Posse Comitatus Act, part of Title XVIII of the U.S. [Government] Code that bars the military from engaging in law enforcement."[59]

The existence of such a law, in any event, did not deter high ranking Reagan administration officials from proceeding with their secret plans. A Pentagon document, "Department of Defense Directive No. 3025.10" dated July 22, 1981, declared:

> In those areas in which martial law has been proclaimed, military resources may be used for local law enforcement. Normally a state of martial law will be proclaimed by the president.
> However, in the absence of such action by the president, a senior military commander may impose martial law in an area of his command where there has been a complete breakdown in the exercise of government functions by local civilian authorities. Military assumption of judicial, law enforcement and administrative functions will continue only so long as necessity of that extreme nature requires interim military intervention.[60]

According to investigative reporter David Lindorff, this martial law directive is still in effect.

Reporter Ron Ridenhour observes that President Reagan had long been fascinated by martial law. Ridenhour secured documents under a 1975 FOIA request which revealed that Mr. Reagan, as governor of California, ran a series of martial law "war games." These "war games" occurred between 1968 and 1972 under the code name "Operation Cable Splicer I, II, and III." They involved California National Guard units, local police, and detachments from the U.S. Sixth Continental Army. The military commander in charge of these operations was National Guard Col. Louis Guiffreda who was named by President Reagan in 1981 to head FEMA. Thus, it was Guiffreda with whom Lt. Col. North worked. The director in charge of Operation Cable Splicer, however, was Governor Reagan's executive secretary, Edwin Meese. At that time, Meese stated that the most important factor in implementing martial law "was advance intelligence gathering to facilitate internment of the leaders of civil disturbances."[61]

As Lindorff phrases it, the Constitution of the United States has no "self-destruct" clause. The only time that martial law can constitutionally be imposed is during war when, and only when, civilian courts are unable to function. But were the Reagan administration's martial law contingency plans anything more than reactionary political fantasies? Under normal circumstances, the answer is no. On at least three occasions in our history, however, the government has, in fact, imposed martial law during times of crisis or "perceived crisis." The one major stain on President Lincoln's otherwise exemplary record was his suspension of the writ of *habeas corpus* in the North. In addition, martial law was imposed in Hawaii after the Japanese attack on Pearl Harbor and, during the Second World War, the government's illegal and unjustified imprisonment of Americans of Japanese ancestry serves as a reminder that fear and hysteria, in times of crisis, can override normal constitutional guarantees. Barring some unforeseen catastrophe, the Reagan administration's contingency plans, which are still in place, undoubtedly will lie dormant. However, the administration's determination to overthrow the Sandinista regime in Nicaragua by military force— regardless of public opinion and congressional opposition—revealed a frightening lack of respect for democratic processes and a willingness to impose its own dark vision on the American people at all costs.

Representative Don Edwards (D-CA), who chairs the House sub-committee on civil liberties and constitutional rights, stated: "I'm deeply disturbed by the reports of martial law planning. We should demand that the whole thing be made public. I had no idea that this kind of thing could go on in this country, but that's where secret government leads you. It is very ominous."[62]

October Surprise

The most important questions that surfaced during the late 1980s, however, dealt not simply with President Reagan's complicity (or lack thereof) in the Iran-Contra scandal, but with unresolved questions and allegations about Mr. Reagan's election campaign in 1980. A number of writers, including Gary Sick and Seymour Hersh, have attempted to unravel the tangled web now referred to as "October Surprise."[63]

The major reason, perhaps, that President Carter lost the election to Mr. Reagan was his inability to resolve the hostage crisis in Iran. Briefly stated, allegations have been made (and are currently being investigated by a congressional committee) that a number of Reagan advisers and associates, including William Casey, cut a deal with Iranian authorities that delayed the release of the American hostages until after the election. Reagan campaign managers, so the story goes, promised to provide Iran with several billion dollars in badly-needed military aid to defend itself in its war with Iraq in return for Iran's agreement not to negotiate further with the Carter administration.

Although most important allegations have yet to be substantiated (and perhaps never will be) we do know, among many other things, that the American hostages in Iran were released within an hour after President Reagan took his oath of office. We also know that in 1981-82, the Israeli government had provided the Iranians with American weapons worth at least $2 billion (and possibly much more). The sale of these weapons to Iran, in short, may well have marked the beginning of the Iran-Contra scandal itself.

The most startling new development about the entire sordid and sorry affair was the indictment of former Secretary of Defense Caspar Weinberger in mid-June 1992 on five counts of perjury stemming from his testimony to Congress. Weinberger's indictment provides an intriguing scenario—not only about his own role in Iran-Contra, but that of former President Reagan and former Vice President Bush. Stay tuned.

The Gulf War

In the amazing world in which we live, new developments and new scandals in both the domestic and international spheres, occur with alarming frequency. Press censorship, media manipulation, and the widespread use of disinformation—practices and techniques pioneered during the invasion of Grenada, refined during the invasion of Panama, and brilliantly executed during the Gulf War, raise serious questions not only about the credibility and integrity of the Reagan and Bush administrations, but about the future course of American history itself.[64]

For example, evidence is now beginning to emerge that strongly suggests that the Bush administration bears primary responsibility for the Gulf War. The war itself was not only extraordinarily costly in monetary terms, but resulted in the deaths of tens of thousands of Iraqi civilians. "High tech" American weapons not only destroyed military targets, but deliberately destroyed every power station, dam, and reservoir in sight. Without electricity and clean water, thousands of Iraqi civilians—men, women, and children—have died, and continue to die from disease. Moreover, the slaughter of the Kurds and Shiite Muslims by elements of Saddam's Republican Guard units that were allowed to escape destruction, is a direct result of the Bush administration's cynicism and disregard for human life. The Kurds in particular, responding to American appeals, rose in arms only to be driven from their homes and slaughtered. Only after extreme pressure from the international community did the Bush administration and its allies belatedly respond to their plight.

Damning evidence has surfaced about the Bush administration's duplicity and indeed, its complicity, in creating the monstrous regime it later tried to destroy. The fact that it supported both Iraq and Iran in their war of attrition is, in terms of international power politics, comprehensible. But once the war was over, at great material and human cost to both sides, the Bush administration continued not only to share intelligence information with the Iraqis, but continued to provide arms and technology to Saddam, and urged other nations around the world to do the same.

In fact, it has come to light that in the months preceding Iraq's invasion of Kuwait, the Bush administration permitted Saddam to utilize $5 billion in agricultural credits for the purchase of additional weapons. Congressional committees are now investigating allegations of collusion by American authorities with Saddam Hussein in the diversion of these funds. If true, the Bush administration, according to congressional sources, is guilty of breaking American law. In any event, it is clear that American efforts to turn Iraq, under Saddam Hussein, into a client state failed, and failed miserably. Never did American authorities attempt to impose limits on Saddam, even after he had used poison gas to kill Kurdish citizens and had uttered threats about his desire to destroy Israel.

Even at the eleventh hour, that is, a few days before Saddam invaded Kuwait, April Glaspie, the American ambassador to Iraq, in commenting on differences between the two countries, informed Saddam that the United States had no intention in getting involved in their border disputes.

Mr. Bush, in the aftermath of the Gulf War, talked vaguely about creating "a new world order." Precisely what he has in mind, and at what cost to the human race in general and the American people in particular, provides little cause for optimism.

Noriega, Panama, and International Kidnapping

Less deadly than the Gulf War in terms of lives lost, but equally important in terms of its implications, was the invasion of Panama, the seizure of General Noriega, and his trial as a "drug lord" in Miami.

Hardly anyone will deny that General Noriega was a dictator and a drug dealer; but the American invasion of a "sovereign" state on the pretense of restoring "democracy" to Panama and combatting narco-terrorism (that is, the international drug traffic) was a serious violation of international law. Or was it? General Noriega's lawyers challenged the right of the United States to try him on drug charges on the grounds that he was a prisoner of war. A federal district judge in Miami ruled, however, that the Panamanian dictator could not use such a defense. Why so? The judge invoked "the vexed *Ker-Frisbie* doctrine to justify his arrest." This doctrine permits American authorities to kidnap criminals overseas and bring them back to the United States for trial without regard for their constitutional rights. As writer Jonathan Stevenson phrases it, the *Ker-Frisbie* "doctrine carries to its logical extreme the anachronistic notion that the Constitution stops at the water's edge." Bruce Zagaris, chairman of the American Bar Association's panel on international criminal law, suggests that this case will do great harm to the integrity of the American judicial system in the long term. How can we preach respect for the rule of law and ask for the release of hostages when we impose our law on another nation?[65]

The invasion of Panama and General Noriega's kidnapping did not cause an international incident because the new Panamanian government was not inclined to lodge a protest. Mexican authorities, however, were not acquiescent when it came to light that American authorities had abducted a Mexican citizen, Dr. Alvarez Machain, in Mexican territory. The doctor had been indicted in the United States for allegedly participating in the kidnapping and murder of an American DEA (Drug Enforcement Agency) agent. The United States and Mexico had an extradition treaty, but Mexican officials wanted to try Dr. Alvarez Machain in Mexican courts and, on several occasions, requested his return.

The case eventually ended up in the United States Supreme Court; and, on June 15, 1992, the Court ruled by a 6-3 majority that the extradition treaty "says nothing about the obligations of the United States and Mexico to refrain from forcible abductions of people from the territory of the other nation. . . ." The decision was written by Chief Justice Rehnquist, and joined by Justices Scalia, Souter, Kennedy, Thomas, and White.

Rehnquist did not deny that "the respondent and his amici" (those who had filed *amicus* briefs on his behalf) might be correct in charging that the doctor's abduction was "in violation of general international law principles." But this, Rehnquist declared, was not the issue the Court had been called upon to decide. The Court's role was to determine whether or not the extradition treaty's language invalidated the Mexican doctor's abduction. Since it clearly did not, it was up to the executive branch, not the Supreme Court, to deal with the outrage of Mexican authorities.

After the Court's decision was announced, the Mexican government filed a protest with the U.S. State Department denouncing once again American "infringement of Mexico's sovereignty." Moreover, Mexico announced that all cooperation with American authorities in attempting to suppress the international drug traffic would cease until Dr. Alvarez Machain was turned over to Mexican authorities for trial.

Secret Laws, Secret Government

Besides death and taxes we can be certain of at least one thing: Whenever the president of the United States waves his magic wand with a "national security" imprint stamped on it, neither the American people nor their elected members in Congress are likely to know anything about it.

President Reagan, for example, issued 298 presidential orders called National Security Decision Directives which are implemented by the National Security Council. Of this number, only the contents of all or a part of thirty are unclassified—including NSDD 84, which we have discussed at length. Even the subject matter of these 268 directives is unknown. A number of critics have observed that nowhere does the Constitution of the United States confer law-making powers on the president; but NSDD's, like executive orders, have the force of law until they are modified or eliminated by the president or his successors."[66] As we have already noted, President Bush has not revoked any important executive orders issued by Mr. Reagan or any of the thirty Reagan NSDDs of which we are aware. Nor do we know precisely how many National Security Directives (Mr. Bush uses a slightly different title) Mr. Reagan's successor has issued. We do know, however, that NSD 26 stifled all criticism by executive branch agencies of continued support of Iraq—including the diversion of credits designated for agricultural purposes to military ones. In short, the imperial presidency, or perhaps we should now call it "The New Leviathan," is rarely held accountable. On occasion, its clandestine activities come to light as they did during the Iran-Contra hearings. Moreover, it is conceivable that, in time, we may learn more about what some congressional sources have referred to as "Iraqgate."

Having said that Congress and the general public have often been victimized by high level executive secrecy, it is also true that Congress, more often than not, has not only failed to challenge foreign policy adventurism by the executive branch, but has virtually abandoned some of its own foreign policy responsibilities. The passage of the 1991 Intelligence Authorization Act provides a case in point.

Under the terms of this law (Public Law 102-88), the president needs only to determine that a covert operation "is necessary to support identifiable foreign policy objectives" and that such action is "important" to the national security of the United States. Under ordinary circumstances, the president is required to inform the congressional intelligence committees of his intention to launch a covert action before it occurs; but this section of the law was rendered meaningless by another provision which allows the president, in the name of national security, to engage in covert operations without prior notification. In this event, the president is required to "inform the intelligence committees in a timely fashion and shall provide a statement of the reasons for not giving prior notice."

Rep. Barbara Boxer (D-CA) introduced an amendment that explicitly challenged presidential authority on covert action. The Boxer Amendment proposed that "no covert operations could be undertaken without notification of and approval by both intelligence committees" and stated that covert action be undertaken only to meet an "extraordinary threat" to the nation's security. The amendment included a provision authorizing the rescue of hostages. But the Boxer Amendment failed by an overwhelming vote of 341-70. Several Members of Congress not only denounced the Boxer Amendment in virulent terms, but suggested that even if such restrictions became law, presidents would probably ignore them anyway. In sum, the mind-set that produced Vietnam, the Iran-Contra affair, the invasions of Grenada and Panama, and the Gulf War is alive and well; and Congress, once again, has willingly acquiesced by agreeing to continue to play the role of junior partner in the conduct of foreign policy.

Epilogue

Not long after the atomic bombs were dropped on Hiroshima and Nagasaki, Albert Einstein remarked that everything had changed except our way of thinking. The collapse of the Soviet empire and the end of the Cold War has produced still another watershed in American and indeed world history. Are we to conclude that Einstein's observation is equally valid today? Or is it possible that, in time, a sufficiently large number of Americans will come to recognize that national security is not linked to maintaining the existence of a Leviathan state, but to the reaffirmation of the principles contained in the Declaration of Independence and the Constitution of the United States—especially the Bill of Rights? Moreover, is it possible that an organic, rather than a static view of law, ethics, and society will help to create a world in which "liberty and justice for all" is more than a platitude uttered, on occasion, by schoolchildren and naturalized citizens? Is America, in historical terms, anything more than a graveyard for utopian experiments? Or can the "better angels of our nature," as Lincoln phrased it, in time prevail?

Suggestions for Additional Reading and a Note on Sources

The most important bibliographical source on censorship during the Reagan era is James R. Bennett's *Control of Information in the United States: An Annotated Bibliography* (Westport, CT: Meckler, 1987). Bennett's *Control of the Media in the United States: An Annotated Bibliography* (New York: Garland, 1992) is also an indispensable guide. My anthology, *Freedom at Risk: Secrecy, Censorship, and Repression in the 1980's* (Philadelphia: Temple Univ. Press, 1988), contains a forty-five page bibliography that deals not only with censorship but with a variety of other themes discussed in this book. *The Alternative Press Index*, however, is a critically important source on the years both before and after 1988. Alternative Press magazines and journals such as *Civil Liberties, In These Times, Mother Jones, The Nation, The Progressive, Utne Reader,* and *Z Magazine* are essential reading.

The *United States Law Weekly* and *The Supreme Court Digest* provide easy access to all court decisions. And the *Congressional Quarterly* provides a critically important guide for anyone attempting to understand and locate materials on the workings of Congress. Moreover, librarians, who specialize in government publications at major public and private libraries, are indispensable in locating and retrieving executive orders, national security directives (those that are not classified, that is), and the staggering number of reports compiled by congressional committees and subcommittees. The *Congressional Record*, of course, is also an essential source for researchers, as are the guidelines issued by all executive branch agencies.

Data Center, located in Oakland, California, publishes annual editions of *The Right to Know*, and provides research assistance in this computer age at a reasonable cost. The National Security Archives in Washington contains important holdings; but its ability to use the FOIA has been crippled. As noted in the text, the Pentagon reclassified the NSA as a commercial user. Unfortunately, the U.S. Circuit Court of Appeals, District of Columbia Circuit, upheld the government's position in July 1989.

Endnotes

[1] For a detailed analysis of countersubversive crusades see Richard O. Curry and Thomas M. Brown, eds., *Conspiracy: The Fear of Subversion in American History* (New York: Holt, Rinehart & Winston, 1972).

[2] In *American Quarterly*, 15 (Summer 1962) and *The Mississippi Valley Historical Review* 48 (September 1960).

[3] Lipset, "The Radical Right: A Problem for American Democracy," *British Journal of Sociology*, 6 (June 1955).

[4] Cole, "McCarran-Walter Act Reborn?" *The Washington Post*, November 18, 1990.

[5] *Ibid.*

[6] Koffler, "The New Seditious Libel," in Richard O. Curry, ed., *Freedom at Risk: Secrecy, Censorship, and Repression in the 1980's* (Philadelphia: Temple Univ. Press, 1988), 148.

[7] Curry, "Introduction," *ibid.*, 11.

[8] Donna A. Demac, *Liberty Denied: The Current Rise of Censorship in America* (New Brunswick, N.J.: Rutgers Univ. Press, 1991), 170.

[9] Curry, "Introduction," *op. cit.*, 12-13.

[10] *Ibid.*

[11] Demac, *op. cit.*, 167-68.

[12] *Ibid.*, 167-68.

[13] See, for example, Vince Passaro, "Funds for the Enfeebled," *Harpers Magazine* (December 1990).

[14] John E. Frohnmayer, "A Portrait of the NEA," *In These Times*, April 8-14, 1992.

[15] Frank Rizzo, "Denial of Arts Funding Decried," *The Hartford Courant*, January 14, 1992.

[16] Paul Mattick, Jr., "Arts and the State," *The Nation*, October 1, 1990.

[17] Ira Glasser, "Artistic Freedom: A Gathering Storm," *Civil Liberties* (Spring 1990), 191.

[18] *Ibid.*

[19] Demac, *op. cit.*, 178.

[20] *Ibid.*, 164-66.

[21] Daniel Ellsberg and Anthony Russo were indicted under the espionage statutes in the Pentagon Papers case in 1972, but charges were dismissed because of government improprieties.

[22] See Steven Burkholder, "The Morison Case: The Leaker As 'Spy,' " in Curry, *Freedom at Risk*, 117-39. This is by far the best analysis yet written on the case.

23 This analysis is based on two of my previously published articles, "Paranoia—Reagan Style: Encounters with the USIA," and "Choices: International Education, Civil Liberties, and Domestic Politics During the 1980's," *ibid.*, 178-202.

24 Geoffrey R. Stone, "The Reagan Administration, the First Amendment, and FBI Domestic Security Investigations," *ibid.*, 273.

25 *Ibid.*, 276-78.

26 *Ibid.*, 278-79.

27 *Ibid.*

28 *Ibid.*, 286.

29 Theoharis, "Conservative Politics and Surveillance: The Cold War, the Reagan Administration, and the FBI," *ibid.*, 259-71; and Autin, "The Reagan Administration and the Freedom of Information Act," *ibid.*, 69-85. On the FBI see also Theoharis and Cox, *The Boss*, Frank Donner, *The Age of Surveillance*, and most recently, Richard Criley, *The FBI v. The First Amendment*.

30 Theoharis, *ibid.*, 269.

31 Curry, "Introduction," *ibid.*, 20.

32 *Ibid.*, 21.

33 *Ibid.*

34 Autin, *ibid.*, 74-75.

35 Curry, *ibid.*, 20-21.

36 Katherine Farrish, "CIA's Visit a Mystery," *The Hartford Courant*, October 26, 1990. See also *Norwich Bulletin*, October 26, 1990.

37 Chip Berlet, "Activists Face Increased Harassment," *Utne Reader* (January/February 1992), 85.

38 Bill McKibben, "Court Jester," *Mother Jones* (November/December 1991), 21.

39 *Ibid.*

40 *Ibid.*

41 NCARL Legislative Alert, "H.R. 50: 'The First Amendment Protection Act.'" Published in 1991.

42 Jamie Kalven, "The Reagan Administration and the Federal Judiciary," in Curry, *op. cit.*, 316.

43 My analysis of Rehnquist's ideas are based on the ACLU's treatment of his judicial philosophy that was published in pamplet form in 1986.

44 Cynthia Garney, "Good-Bye, *Roe v. Wade?*" *The Washington Post National Weekly Edition*, March 2-8, 1992. Garney essay is astute and highly recommended.

45 *The New York Times*, June 30, 1992.

46 Gina Kolata, "Ruling Inspires Groups to Fight Harder," *ibid.*, June 30, 1992.

47 Reprinted from the *Los Angeles Times* in the *Hartford Courant*, July 2, 1992.

48 See particularly Linda Greenhouse "Revealing View of Court," *New York Times*, July 2, 1992.

49 "Public Enemy Number One," *The Progressive* (August 1991).

50 Linda Greenhouse, "New Term to Test Supreme Court's New Majority," *The New York Times*, October 6, 1991.

51 Robert Pear, "With Rights Act Comes Fight to Clarify Congress's Intent," *ibid.*, November 17, 1991.

52 *Ibid.*

53 Ruth Marcus, "A Civil Rights Bill to Satisfy No-one," *The Washington Post National Weekly Edition*, November 4-10, 1991.

54 Steven Holmes, "Lawyers Expect Ambiguities," *The New York Times*, December 27, 1991.

55 Curry, "Introduction," *op. cit.*, 26.

[56] *Ibid.*

[57] *Ibid.*, 26-27.

[58] *Ibid.*, 27.

[59] *Ibid.*

[60] *Ibid.*, 28.

[61] *Ibid.*

[62] *Ibid.*, 29.

[63] Gary Sick, "The Election Story of the Decade," *The New York Times*, April 15, 1991.

[64] Stanley W. Cloud, "On a Tight Leash: Journalists Assail the Pentagon Pool System," *Time*, January 8, 1990.

[65] Jonathan Stevenson, "Noriega Has Been Denied a Constitutional Right," *In These Times*, Nov. 27-Dec. 10., 1991.

[66] Angus MacKenzie and Eve Pell, "Secret Laws of Reagan-Bush, *The Hartford Advocate*, October 24, 1988.

EDUCATIONAL PROJECTS
of the
FIRST AMENDMENT FOUNDATION

The Foundation has provided funding for a variety of educational projects, including the following:

- **Film: "The Vigil: Remembering Lovejoy"**
  A documentary/drama film on Reverend Elijah Lovejoy, this nation's first martyr to the cause of a free press.

- **Black Voter's Harassment**
  An educational pamphlet by Anne Braden, entitled: "The FBI vs. Black Voting Rights"—a case study of recent FBI intimidations of Black voters and voting rights activists in Alabama.

- **Seminar on "Political Dissent and the Law"**
  Featuring civil liberties specialists with experience dealing with governmental intimidations of individuals' and organizations' free speech rights (March 1986 at Loyola Law School, Los Angeles).

- **Research Project: "The FBI's 'Neutralization' Program"**
  Ten-year research program to decipher, analyze and classify 132,000 pages of political surveillance and disruption, obtained through an ACLU lawsuit (*Wilkinson v. FBI*), of the FBI's attempt to "neutralize" the First Amendment activities of the National Committee Against Repressive Legislation (NCARL).

- **Pamphlet: "Political Smears—A Technique for Suppression"**
  A grant to the Bill of Rights Foundation in Chicago for publishing a series of essays by civil libertarians explaining the purpose and use of the political smear technique in the McCarthy era ("Red-Baiting," etc.)

- **Book: "The FBI v. The First Amendment" by Richard Criley**
  How the FBI under the direction of J. Edgar Hoover unsuccessfully attempted to "neutralize" a civil liberties organization. How the FBI continues to violate First Amendment rights under the Reagan/Bush secret FBI "guidelines."

  Note: Foreword by Henry Steele Commager—Cartoons, permission of Paul Conrad, *L.A. Times*—Author Richard Criley, received an award from The Fund of Free Expression's Lillian Hellman/Dashiell Hammett Legacy.

- **Monograph: "At War With Peace: U.S. Covert Operations"**
  Summarizing the history and covert operations of the Central Intelligence Agency (CIA), 1947-1990.

- **First Amendment Monitoring Service**
  "The Right to Know & The Freedom to Act"—A bi-monthly publication reporting First Amendment vilations by the three branches of the federal government, and, the private/voluntary sector.

- **Conference Handbook**
  "News Clippings and Documents: A History of FBI Abuses Past and Present," prepared for the: "*FBI v. First Amendment—A National Conference*," Washington, D.C., October 10-12, 1991.

- **Tribute to THOMAS I. EMERSON—1907-1991**
  Lines Professor of Law—Yale University; founding member of the First Amendment Foundation's Board of Directors.
  Honoring his contributions as: An authority on the First Amendment—A civil liberties and civil rights activist—A pioneer for women's equality.

The FIRST AMENDMENT FOUNDATION Needs Your Help to Achieve the Widest Possible Distribution of this Educational Book:

- Obtain your copy and copies to give to your friends
- Contribute generously to help us distribute the book to students, libraries, and groups unaware of the danger to their rights

Suggested contribution:

Single Copy: $12.00
(If ordering by mail, add $3.00)

BULK ORDERS

10 copies: (10% discount) $108.00

20 copies: (20% discount) $192.00

30 copies: (30% discount) $252.00

40 copies: (40% discount) $288.00

(If ordering 10 or more copies by mail add $1.00 per copy plus UPS charges)

Make checks payable to the FIRST AMENDMENT FOUNDATION

Contributions are Tax Deductible.
Approved, Internal Revenue Service Tax Exemption, Sec. 501(c)(3)
I.D. 95–3922815

FIRST AMENDMENT FOUNDATION
1313 West 8th Street—Suite 313
Los Angeles, California 90017

(213) 484-6661 — FAX (213) 484-0266